Conte

Before we begin....

Imagine, walking into a concert stadium before a gig. It's huge. It's full. It's dark. It's loud. There's excitement in the air..... Something is about to happen - something BIG. More and more people are arriving to the stadium and adding to the throng of expectancy, the buzz is almost palpable. There are waves of noise coming from areas outside of your vision, groups of revellers having the time of their lives, a little bit of fear creeps in. Then, darkness. The Headliner arrives on stage. The whole place erupts and blows the roof off! Cheers, claps, whoops, noise, music, lights, movement. You look around, everyone is on their feet in united joy! It feels euphoric! It's happening! The main event has arrived!

This is a 'hair on the back of your neck' moment. When that headliner walks on stage and all aspects of this well planned and rehearsed event come together, it is truly impressive.

Behind the scenes somewhere there will be the headliners manager - closely monitoring and checking all pieces of this huge occasion are working, having been integral to the success of this monumental masterpiece. The manager is not distracted by the sheer magnitude of this event nor are they taking part in it. They are simply calm in a chaotic environment.

I'm pretty sure there aren't many people in the concert stadium who are thinking about, or are even aware of the Headliner Manager. But without this integral internal cog in this well oiled machine, it would simply stop working. The planner who is there who sees everything, knows everything, feels everything.

The role of a Personal Assistant to a Headteacher or Senior Leader in any form, is one very similar to that of the Headline Manager. The role is full of variables. No two days are the same and no two leaders are the same. However there are some very clear and practical principles of the PA role that ring true for almost all who hold this post, and there are some pragmatic and imaginative ways in which a PA can support their leader to be successful, while also fulfilling their own need for a job 'well done'. Likewise, the role doesn't come with an automatic halo! You as a PA will need to tread a fine line of getting the best out of yourself and your Headteacher, and keeping your own well being in check.

Who do you think you are?

Do we need PAs to Headteachers within education? This is a relatively new role within education, but in essence people have been doing many of the tasks mentioned in this book for years. Until recently the person doing all of this may have just been called the school secretary! This has evolved to office or admin manager over time but as our schools became more complex and more like businesses these roles have become confusing. Also what is expected of a headteacher now is vastly different to 20 years ago. There is far more strategy, admin and organisation for leaders and it is probably going to increase further.

To this end it makes sense to think differently and change how schools operate on the admin side. We can't think like we used to, as schools are a different place now. However there will still be a lot of push backs to a Headteacher having a PA, especially with budgets being so tight. They may well get a feeling of 'Who do you think you are, having a PA!' from others around them.

I haven't really answered my own question. In short, yes we do need PAs to the Headteacher within education. If we want to allow Headteachers to work at their very best, having a PA is the road to that happening. Being a PA to the Headteacher (or CEO or group of SLT) will allow those people to function at a far greater depth than if they didn't have one. And the end result of that will be better outcomes for the students.

Can every school afford one? No. So what then? As I've said above, although some of what a PA does is new in the ever changing landscape of education, some of these roles, tasks, jobs have been done for donkey's years. Do you need to be called a PA to do them? Again no. But does it help? Absolutely! But why?

Does it matter what you are called?

I've championed for years for support and admin staff to be given more respect within our profession and the wider world. Pay is a small part of that, recognition is much bigger. Job titles are powerful when it comes to respect. We could probably argue that they shouldn't be, but let's work with the world we live in. I'm not saying that the titles of School Secretary or Office Manager are wrong, but do they do the role you do justice? Could you tweak it to reward you for all that you do? Or even ask for a job re-evaluation. If you have been in your role for a while, the chances are it has changed a lot since you started. Not only does this help with the respect for the work that you do, it protects you in the future against any organisational changes.

It's also important to discuss where you sit within the roles and responsibilities of the school. Knowing where you are, who you answer to, who you support and more importantly - who you don't, is vital for your boundaries. But it can really also help for the level of respect you get from your colleagues and from people outside of school.

You may be worried that doing this may mean even more work for you, or if you are reading this coming newly into an advertised role of PA to the Headteacher that you have taken on too much. Especially as very often a job description will have something along the lines of 'and anything else the Headteacher directs you to' sentence.

It is very hard to define the role of a PA. Although we pull on Jo's experiences in this book, we also know they are very limited to the school and area she has worked in and have therefore done lots of research to give you a well rounded overview.

So what do they actually do?

Most importantly - assist the Headteacher to be the best Headteacher they can be, but that is horribly vague! And a good PA does not like vague, they like specifics.

A very basic summary of Jo's tasks are as follows

- Organisational tasks - diary keeping, messages, arranging appointments, phone calls
- Communication tasks - phone calls, email management, writing bespoke letters and emails
- Project planning work - researching and booking trips including travel and accommodation, special events (recruitment, special visits, media and 3rd party coverage)
- For the Head - write on their behalf, liaise with stakeholders (from students to Trustees and everything in between), be their 'eyes and ears' around the school, be a critical friend and a wellbeing monitor.

- Compliance tasks - oversee complaints, student suspensions, Permanent Exclusions, oversee school policy management.
- Meetings - organise and attend as needed - complex minute taking and advise on guidance and expectations.
- Provide structure for the Headteacher and be their gatekeeper.
- Ordering and purchasing on behalf of the school (including bespoke designs of items).
- Manage the demands of the Head and other senior leaders.
- Line Manage other members of support staff.
- Liaison between internal departments (finance, HR, Facilities, central teams).
- Marketing the school, including events and social media.

But as her role evolves, she is learning that some of these tasks don't have to be or shouldn't be done by her and you will find the same. Some have fallen to her because no one else was doing them. She took them on but is now either delegating them out to someone better suited, or putting structures in place to allow others to easily pick them up as and when they are needed.

A good example of that is PEX pack reports. They hadn't been done at her school before, so when they had the first incident of one needing to be done, Jo swooped in. But she is now working on a proforma and delegation system where others can come in and do some parts of it using documents she has created. This helps her workload and wellbeing but also fosters a sense of teamwork around what can be a stressful task.

As you navigate your way through being a PA, or adopting some parts of a PAs role into your existing job you can do the same. Embrace the power of imperfect action, get it done so it's gone off your list. But then use the power of reflection to learn and grow moving forward.

Who do you think you are? - Blinking amazing, that's what!

1

The 5 PA Principles

In this book you will find a host of information on how to become a great PA, to anyone, based around the 5 PA Principles: how to support your leader to be the best they can be, and how to fulfil your own goals and ambitions, while maintaining your personal standards and most importantly your wellbeing. You will learn what to do to prepare for visitors and inspections, how that compares to real life. You'll gain knowledge on how to build relationships with your leader and how your role as their PA is a unique and crucial part of their success. You will find advice on how to deal with new and difficult situations and overcome them. You will also find ways to find your own sense of 'job well done' and strategies on how to run the day to day workings of your leaders expectations.

The 5 PA principles are simple but effective rules to live by. By embracing these principles you and your leader can flourish, helping your school to be the very best it can be.

Definition:

A 'principle' is a kind of rule, belief or idea that guides you. In general, a principle is some kind of basic truth that helps you with your life.

 1   The tools to be prepared

Having that pivotal 'thing' at the right time. An example of this is my trusted 'magic pad'. Now, as much as I would like it to be, the pad itself is not magic! Almost like a Police Constable's note book, everything gets noted in the pad. It is an A4 spiralled lined book split into 4 sections using simple bulldog clips (you don't need anything fancy or expensive). I take my pad everywhere with me. And I mean everywhere! I rely on it to make a note at any time, especially when I'm not at my desk. I will get daily bits of information that need to be acted upon, sometimes just as a verbal request, while passing someone in the corridor that I write down. Flashes of brilliance, ideas from your Headteacher, observations from around school, students names all get noted if needed. This has also served as a brilliant reminder of things I need to do or have been done, and allows me to avoid forgetting context. As an example, I keep all my old notebooks in a particular job - and have used them to go back and check information I have written down or instructions someone has given me should it be queried later on.

Magic Pad Section 1 is all the previous days you've completed in a bulldog clip so they don't flap about.

Magic Pad Section 2 is today and blank pages in a bulldog clip. At the start of each day, begin a new page and write the date on it. Write down your to-do list for that day, including anything you didn't get to from yesterday.

Magic Pad Section 3 is any project notes you're working on that aren't finished in a day

Magic Pad Section 4 at the back is for a loose bit of paper that you inevitably get given throughout the day or term that you'd like to keep or reference.

Another item that I can't do without is a small black cross body shoulder pouch/bag. It's slightly bigger than an A6 piece of paper, not fancy or expensive. I wear it at all times so aside from my pad, I can be hands free (usually to open doors or use my lanyard). In it I carry several essentials. My phone (I use this every single day to take photos of amazing things around the school to share with SLT or on our newsletter, plus for emergencies), some pens and a highlighter, a packet of mints, a post it pad (to write notes for students) and any other small thing I need for the day. When I'm on duty I clip my radio to it so it's easily accessible and not in my hand.

2   Fail to plan, plan to fail

This is a well known phrase and very relevant! As a PA, it's your job to think of things no one else has considered, to anticipate the unexpected, and to have a plan! A few good examples of this are in the 'Ofsted' section of this book, the principles are the same in any setting.

Recruitment and interviewing require a great deal of thought and require a plethora of different people to make it work. I tend to try to work backwards in this situation to form a plan. If you want to appoint a candidate by a certain day (the interview day) this will be your starting point. Work backwards from here -

say a week to allow candidates to prepare and notify their employers. Then from there, allow time for the interview panel to shortlist candidates (depending on the availability of who is interviewing) possibly 3 days maximum. This will allow you time to print off the completed application forms for scrutiny. Be aware, some positions will be very popular so could have in excess of 20 applicants. From there, go backwards to allow as much time as possible for candidates to make their applications. Where possible I allow for 2 weekends to sit within this time, or longer for senior roles. This will give you a date for when the job has to start to be advertised internally and externally as needed. This adds up to about 4 weeks! Before all this can happen, the role itself needs to be confirmed, vetted, and ready to advertise.

1	Headteacher or lead recruiter to decide on who will conduct the interviews and their availability. Decide on the interview date, vacancy itself, salary, and times. Applications open and advertising goes out	Variable time depending on whether the adverts and applications are ready to go live. Allow a 2 week window before closing where possible. Start prepping - rooming, staffing, parking
2	Applications close, shortlisting and candidate invites. 1 week before interview day.	Continue prepping! Interview questions, Feedback forms and scoring, Tasks, students, Lunch and refreshments, Safeguarding for candidates to move around the school
3	Interview (appointment day)	Health and Safety, Safeguarding, access arrangements

For teaching staff, this is doable, as they are required to give a full term's notice however bear in mind that the person you will end up recruiting will also need to give a full term of notice too!

Once these wheels are in motion, you can start thinking about and planning the actual interview day. While as PA you may not be on the main interview panel, you may well be invited to oversee some of the interview days (the one I set up for our current Headteacher was 2 full days of tasks followed by his formal interview!) As you can imagine, there are lots of plates to spin here but with the right planning, you can get everyone on board, in the right places at the right times for it to run smoothly.

When you know how many candidates you will be holding interviews for, and for senior positions, each task and panel interviewer will need a 'pack' so they know what they need to do and when, including feedback, scoring, rooming, any IT requirements and access arrangements. Don't leave anything to the last minute (allow yourself a day for the printer to not work!).

In amongst all this, be ready to adjust your plans! Staff might be unwell, a room might be double booked, a candidate may be late or not turn up, you may need to supply a vegan lunch at the last minute ..... Any number of things! My advice is to stay calm and do what you can to overcome any hiccups.

This method can be adopted for almost any situation or event. If the King visits the school, parents evening, Summer Fayre - the thinking behind the event will be the same or very similar!

Your Headteacher and Senior Leaders will know and trust that their day/event will be successful if you've prepared and planned it, allowing them to concentrate on what they need to do.

3   Wellbeing

You need to be at your best, that's a simple but very important fact. This job is demanding at the best of times, overwhelming and exhausting at its worst. So you need to take responsibility for being at your best and that means prioritising your wellbeing and learning how to have that as one of your core principles.

This feeds into every other point. If you are tired you will forget your magic pad, if you are anxious you will take words personally, if you are ill you will forget to plan ahead, stress is like kryptonite for your ninja skills.

It will go against every bone in your body to put yourself first, but it's a skill you need to master. But there is a second element to this, helping your leader to protect their wellbeing too. They need to do it for the same reasons you do, but they probably need a lot of help to get there. As the gatekeeper to their life you have the unique power to not only lead by example, but be practical about making it happen for them.

To do this you need to learn about wellbeing, what it actually is and how work affects our wellbeing. The synergy between your wellbeing and that of others is complex, but the answers are later in this book.

4   It's not personal

Sounds simple enough! Anything that is worth doing, is worth doing properly. For me, this means giving my all to my role and doing the best that I can. Life as a PA can be so very rewarding and I would not want to do much else - however, there are times when the intensity of a role so close to the Headteacher can be overwhelming especially if the school is facing high stakes situations (a permanent exclusion, complaints, dip in exam results). During these times, or when you or your Headteacher are experiencing issues outside of school, your emotions and nerves may be stretched which is completely normal for a human being! Be kind to yourself, and to each other - and remember whatever you're experiencing, it's not personal in a professional environment. The chances are, you're both doing your absolute best under whatever circumstances you find yourselves in, and you're actually doing a great job! Take a breath, go for a walk, and clear your head. If something is niggling at you, it's best to address it and draw a line. It will make you both stronger as individuals and as a team of your very own.

5   Secret Superhero Ninja

Yes - you! One principle that must never be forgotten, is your true self. All the things you do, think about, think more about, decide and cogitate, amount up to an amazing secret superhero ninja PA! Remember that this is what makes you amazing at your job. The unnoticed little things (or sometimes greatly noticed and appreciated things) like, but not limited to:

- remembering that a certain visitor to school like Pepsi Max,
- knowing your Headteacher likes Earl Grey tea in the afternoon,
- printing off a document before you're even asked,
- opening all the windows before anyone arrives,
- washing up over 20 dirty mugs after a long day,
- smiling when you're shattered
- asking - what can I do for you? How can I help you today?

- turning off the lights
- giving and sharing positivity and credit
- listening
- maximum integrity, trust and discretion

Remember that you are your own superhero too. When you tell others they're doing a great job, tell yourself that too. Kindness is free and it is important you use it in abundance for yourself and others. The culture you help to build will be priceless and will aid your Headteacher and yourself to leave a lasting legacy for the school, staff and students.

2

Hello! Jo Deane

I haven't always been a PA! But my job roles (in whatever capacity) have shaped who I am and how I function as an adult, in addition to life and family experiences. It's all encompassing. Everything that happens in life will add a layer of information to your wealth of experience. While it is sensible to try to have a line between your personal and your professional life, it is almost impossible to achieve as you are intrinsically linked to both and one can so greatly affect the other. The phrase 'I didn't get where I am today without.....' rings true for so many facets of anyone's career. So it's important not to address any one thing in isolation, but to understand what got you there and why.

My first 20 years of adulthood saw me working and studying in the Financial Services industry in Bristol, I finished college at 17, and by my 18th birthday I was working full time for a Financial Services giant. My role was as junior as it could be, in the Life Cover Quotes Team. I didn't really love it or hate it. I was living at home with my amazing Mum and Dad and my boyfriend and I were saving for a house and wedding. Yes, we were young and had met when I was 15 and he was 16, but he was the 'One'. Fast forward to when I was 27; we had been married for 7 years and I was expecting our first baby. My job at this time was Support Team Manager at another Financial Services giant. I had a team of about 20 people plus a handful of temps at its fullest. The job was stressful and out of 7 leaders, I was the only female in the large department. This didn't particularly affect me at the time as I had never known any different. There was a certain level of sexism, but it 'came with the territory' and was widely accepted as the norm. The Financial Services industry bigwigs in the 1990's/2000's was a male dominated zone. Sales teams were made up of mostly men and my Support Team was a mix of genders but the balance was more men. The difference here was that the men in my team really saw their jobs as a stepping stone to something else, whereas the women in the team were longstanding and experienced. Again, I neither loved it nor hated it at the time, (looking back I actually didn't enjoy the environment at all), but my sights were set on having a family so I knew things would hopefully change soon.

I was over the moon that not long after deciding to start a family, I became pregnant. However, during the early stages of my pregnancy, I was under a lot of stress and pressure - I was in the middle of exiting a member of staff via a disciplinary procedure and I was the direct line manager. As is the way, home life was in a good place however the workload in the office was mounting. I've never enjoyed confrontation of any kind and found face to face 'difficult' conversations a cause for more than butterflies in my stomach! I knew part of being a leader and manager of over 20 colleagues was to fulfil my duties no matter how difficult they were. Life just carried on and no-one but a few trusted friends knew I was pregnant. It was like I had my own little secret and it acted as a kind of shield that there was more to life than the disciplinary procedure I had to follow. I was happy!

In those days, the policies in place for grievances and disciplinary procedures didn't encompass a huge amount of detail and even though there was a Human Resources department and plenty of resources, no training was given about how to deal with difficult situations and how to ensure clauses are upheld. After weeks and months of going through performance plans and reviews, the situation had got to a point where the individual had to be dismissed. The individual who was being exited appealed the case - and won. They came back to the office months later (on full pay and benefits) in a different team, albeit a stone's throw from my team. We bumped into each other each and every day.

Sadly, as I went for my first pregnancy scan at St Michael's Hospital in Bristol, I knew something was up. I was 13 weeks pregnant and just couldn't put my finger on what was wrong. I certainly looked and felt pregnant (I showed immediately!) The sonographer got to work and I led there being 'probed' with a full bladder. Then the words 'I'm so sorry, there's no heartbeat' were heard in that little dark room. It felt like time slowed down to a snail's pace in an instant. A brain fog descended and I had to get myself sorted out and go and wait in the 'early pregnancy clinic' downstairs, where they played Radio 2 and Terry Wogan. Unfortunately I sat there with at least 6 other women who were clearly going through the same situation (or worse) as me. I thought: this must be the most depressing room in the world. I got called through by another nurse, male, who had to give me my options and describe to me what might happen to my body and hormones over the next 2 weeks. I think he was actually more nervous than me.

Nature took its course over the next few days and I was signed off work for 2 weeks to recover. Even though my body wasn't pregnant anymore, I felt like a zombie. And I still LOOKED pregnant. The pregnancy hormones were still raging in my body even though there was no baby. When I returned to work, I had a letter in my emails with my annual bonus and pay review for the financial year in arrears. I opened it to find no bonus and the minimum pay increase in line with National Average Earnings. I didn't quite understand? Did I miss a cut off? Was there a mistake? I queried this with my line manager who confirmed, there was not a mistake and the letter reflects an appropriate pay review as I had had 2 weeks off sick. I couldn't believe it! I felt so vulnerable. I felt that a piece of my soul had been taken away and I was still very much in mourning after the miscarriage. I toyed with just letting it go. Was it worth facing up to the bosses in work with the risk I could come away feeling worse than I already did? What if they simply laughed at me or referred me to another department? What if this dragged on for weeks or months? Did I have the physical and emotional energy for that? Would I just end up getting upset in front of those I was desperate to not cry in front of? To perhaps just let the situation go unchallenged was not cowardice but self preservation. If I wanted to keep my job and my potential maternity benefits, should I rock the boat? Hmmm. Yes, it felt like the right thing (not the easy thing) to do.

I gathered up as much strength as possible to query this with the Area Manager. I was still heartbroken about the loss I had just endured but if I could just show that this was not right, I would have no regrets. The one thing I hadn't accounted for was not being able to say the word 'miscarriage'. My brain was protecting me from the reality of it. I went along to the area managers office to state my case. To be fair, he backed down pretty quickly for which I was grateful but I was so angry! How many other women had put up with this through no fault of their own!? If I had not questioned this, it would have not been amended. My immediate manager and my Area manager must have both approved the bonuses so in their minds, they must have considered it fair. I felt so cheated. These people were supposed to be my role models and I had worked so hard to get to where I was. I was really crushed there and then, I knew they didn't have my 'back'. It crossed my mind that now they knew I was planning a family, to the business, I simply wasn't worth being treated with fairness and kindness. If our family plans went well, I would be going on maternity leave within a year. There were other things niggling in the back of my mind - there were no females on the Leadership Team. I didn't feel there was anyone I could reach out to and confide in and now everyone knew my family plans, the cat was out of the bag. And what if I couldn't actually carry a child to full term? I needed to have my career as a stable frontier in my life - for now.

Even though this was not a pleasant time in my life, I did learn a hell of a lot about the reality of management (right or wrong) and being a female in what felt like a man's world (contrasting to teaching and school roles which are female dominated except for senior positions). Specifically, I learnt that I needed to back myself as in this work environment, no-one else was going to do it for me. I had to stand up for what I thought was right, even if it felt uncomfortable, not just for myself, but for anyone else who might find themselves in a similar situation in the future. I learnt to choose my battles, being able to weigh up the pro's and con's of challenging ideas and decisions and when. This was mostly for my own wellbeing as there were still things that were non-negotiable. My mental health, my salary, my benefits, my potential family. These things had to come first. Even though in a society where some employers and individuals will bank on this being the case for so many, (so they can keep their idea of the status quo), I knew this path was right for me at this time.

Time ticked on and within the next 8 years, we moved house, and I thankfully had 2 successful pregnancies and births. The kids were in Primary school and I was working part-time (3 days a week) in a small Independent Financial Planning practice in the centre of Bristol. I loved that job! Not because it was in Financial Services, but because I worked with amazing people and I was 'front of house'. I essentially was the face of the business when our clients walked in. I managed all sorts of work and built up a reputation for being meticulous with detail. Also, my immediate boss was a woman who had a family while also being a partner in the business. At last a female role model! She was a breath of fresh air, and it was the first time I felt truly appreciated for what I could offer. I was also Treasurer of my children's school PTA and enjoyed a lot of success doing this alongside working 3 days a week. Life was good. I had no idea that the Treasurer role at school would be my unofficial 'in' to working within a school, albeit an unpaid role.

Then Spring 2014 came and I was due a routine smear test. All my other tests over the years had been normal so I casually went along for the procedure without a great deal of concern. However, 2 weeks later things started to unravel. They had found pre-cancerous cells in my smear test - severe CIN3. I was one step away from cervical cancer. As the worst year of my life unfolded I became a bystander to my own world. I had several procedures and tests confirming that things were not great and I was offered a hysterectomy. I was 34. To be honest, I jumped at the chance to get this 'risk to life' organ out of my body. I thankfully didn't have cancer but I was far too close to it. My work was absolutely amazing during this time and I was able to use the company private health insurance to have the operation as soon as possible. I needed 6 weeks off and a phased return to work and life was looking like it was getting normal again,

Unfortunately this didn't last long and within another 6 weeks I was back in hospital as the incisions inside my body had ruptured and my healthy organs were trying to escape! After another (emergency) operation and another 2 weeks off from work, I was back on my feet. Thank goodness. As my body started healing again, I was starting to feel aches and pains that were not supposed to be there. Back and forth to hospitals, doctor's appointments and specialists over a 6 week period and there wasn't a clear theory on what the constant pain was. I fell into a deep depression that I could only get out of with the help of medication. Again, my work and my boss in particular were amazing. They made it so that I didn't feel any pressure about returning before I was ready and allowed me the time I needed to get better without judgement. It was my silver lining.

I was on strong painkillers for a long time but slowly my body began to regain strength and confidence. My family, especially my husband, got me through this. I will forever be in their debt.

Not long after this, in 2015, my son was diagnosed with Dyslexia and Developmental Language Disorder, and (entirely separately) my husband started his own business. It felt like the universe was telling me to step away from my job and concentrate on my family. So I did. Fortunately we were in a position where we had enough savings to carry me through for a while so I took the plunge. I essentially began my first PA role as admin and finance (and tax and general do everything person) for my husband's business in Autumn 2015.

I continued my work with my kids school as PTA Treasurer and was really enjoying being part of school life. I was a familiar face and volunteered in my kids classes as a parent-reader and helped the Teaching Assistants work load so they could concentrate on working with the kids rather than photocopying and glueing! Within a few weeks of sorting out my husband's (endless) paperwork and PTA work, the Headteacher of the school asked if I could help clerk a Full Governors Meeting as the current clerk had stepped away. It was supposed to be a one-off favour and to be honest I jumped at the chance (I was already DBS Checked).. He said I would be paid for the time and I would also get to meet the Governing Board. I was very excited! One meeting led to another and within a month I was the official clerk with a contract and a proper salary.

It felt like an unexpected prize from the universe. I thought, I'm going to roll with this and see where it takes me. I was open to new things and continued being the PTA Treasurer too. I had built up a positive relationship with the Headteacher and Deputy Head and I felt like I was being useful towards something bigger than just me. Once again, the Headteacher approached me for a favour - another local school was struggling with office support due to long term absence and would I be open to a call from their Head to perhaps agree to some casual admin work to help them get on top of their workload? Of course the answer was Yes!

I got to work with the office staff, deal with children and parents, cover the phones and really make a difference to young people's lives. What started off as a few hours turned into as many hours as I wanted on a casual basis. This meant I could maintain my duties as a clerk, still help my husband and be a mum. Win:win:win. This was also where I had my first experience of Ofsted. Inspections in Primary schools, Secondary schools and other education settings all vary! Life continued on like this for a few years including during the Covid 19 lockdowns. I had lots of fingers in lots of pies and gained so much experience along the way. I was dealing with every level of school life from 4 year old starters to 16 year old leavers, teachers, leaders, support staff, parents, Governors and trustees. All at the same time! And I loved it.

Becoming a PA

What is probably obvious here, is that I didn't have a clear career path. There is no way I could have engineered for all this to happen at once, but transitioning from private sector work to public sector was actually perfectly doable if you are open to the opportunities that are out there. I firmly believe that if you are unfulfilled in your career, there will be something else out there for you. It might not be straight away, but if you put yourself in situations where you are open to new opportunities, you will find them. If you are interested in a certain industry or job, seek it out. Like me, you will find your transferable skills are actually universal to any type of role. Think about it. The only other element that is truly replicated in any job you do, is YOU. Be your own superhero. People anywhere will buy into YOU. No matter where you are or what your goals are. If YOU believe in yourself and have the self worth to know you have something to offer, employers and leaders will be able to see this through any CV, application form or letter.

Seeking out voluntary roles is a great way to get a foot in the door anywhere. Most schools would be very appreciative of a parent or grandparent helper. From reading with 5 year olds, to utilising your skills as a promoter, there will be something you can offer. Build relationships, spread the word that you'd be interested in anything permanent that came along. Meanwhile, do research on what type of additional skills you could attain in your pursuit of something new. Perhaps something as simple as an online typing course, or a first aid certificate! There are numerous qualifications available to anyone who wants to learn about being a PA (or indeed any vocation). Once you start looking, more and more avenues will open up. An exciting time indeed!

Connect with me!

X	@paprinciples @jojo_deane
f	@ThePAPrinciples
⊙	@the.pa.principles
in	Joanne Deane
✉	paprinciples@gmail.com

3

Hello! Kimberley Evans

I've never had the job of a PA, and by that I mean no one has ever paid me to be a PA. But organising and facilitating other people to shine is one of my superpowers. Over the years I have done many of the roles of a PA under many guises and developed my skills of listening, noticing, working hard for others and standing back.

These were skills passed down from my parents as you'll see when you read on, (much is probably in my DNA to be honest) learnt by watching them lead full, exciting lives volunteering for many organisations alongside busy jobs. A friend once said to me, "I've learnt that if you ever want something done, ask a busy person. They are the best people to get it done right and properly!" Just like being a great teacher is in your blood, I think organising is too. You can learn certain skills to perfect your craft along the way, but I do think many people are just born with it in them. You'll see why when I tell you a bit about my parents!

My dad had a high powered job in logistics which saw him working away from home a lot. In my teenage years it was pretty normal for him to leave on a flight early on Monday morning and not be home until Friday evening. Or be on work phone calls late into the evening as he was communicating with teams in different time zones. Yet, alongside that he found the time to volunteer with organisations that mattered to the family and I spent many wonderful hours flipping burgers alongside him raising money for the Scouts, delighting in the fact that he was home..

My mum had a similar route into her job as Jo! She had a background in banking, but gave up work to look after me and my brother. But just because she didn't have a paid job, she certainly worked hard. Volunteering at all of the schools we went to, through reading with pupils to organising PTA events, being on the WI, she was a Girl Guide leader, my leader in fact so I saw her wonderful organisation close up, By the time I was at secondary school she was ready to go back to work and found the perfect job for her skills, the local primary school *secretary*. I've put that in italics as looking back now, it was so much more than that. That was her official job title, but her role encompassed what is now secretary, business manager, finance officer and PA. It was a small, one form entry school and just like many small schools, she was the only one doing all those things. The same school now has 3 separate roles for this. My mum is also a serial committee member, I worry that she is addicted sometimes! Since retiring from her paid job she is actually often even busier and at one point got up to the heady heights of sitting on 13 different committees at the same time! She is currently Chair of Governors for both the primary school and secondary schools that me and my brother attended, (we are both now well into our 40s, so left a long time ago!) but has thankfully worked on a succession plan so she can retire from those this year. I'm betting though that by the time this book gets published she will have found another project to get involved in!

You'll see soon how this all fits in with me and how my life panned out.

My actual job roles have been very different to Jo's. I qualified as a teacher in 1999, and taught various year groups before leaving to have my children. Like Jo, I had been volunteering in my daughters' school and was Co-Chair of the PTA. The Headteacher knew me and my background and approached me with a job. It was 5 weeks after my youngest had started school, I was looking forward to finally getting all those jobs done at home that you can't do with a toddler and preschooler around!

But when he asked me to apply for a temporary TA role, those household jobs were again put on the back burner as that turned into a permanent TA position and then into a HLTA role, working 3 days a week. For years I loved that job, I said it was like 'playing at being a teacher', as I got to do all the great stuff; making a difference to children's lives, teaching exciting lessons and being creative with resources and displays, without all the tasks that zap teachers' enthusiasm like assessments, report writing and parents evenings. I was also able to use my organisational skills to the max, I saw problems and solved them before others realised there was an issue, helped teachers and other staff work to their best potential by keeping things neat and organised.

Not being a 'proper' teacher suited me wonderfully, our eldest daughter was diagnosed with Autism and ADHD at age 9. It was a difficult time because although I loved working at the same school as my children, that did create problems when certain staff weren't being supportive with our requests for help with our daughter. I needed to be more present at home and I couldn't do that and be a 'proper teacher' at the same time. There were too many, more important, demands on my time.

I did however jump at the chance of another part time job at Leeds Castle in the Education Department. My degree was in history with education and this was a particular area of interest to me. A family friend who also worked there got in touch and said, "I don't know if now is the right time, but there is a job vacancy for an Education Assistant and they don't come along very often!" It was totally not the right time in my life, but I knew I had to grab the chance whilst it was there and I have never regretted it! I love the variety it brings to my week, with different schools and ages coming each day, every day is completely different, and having a 900 year old castle as your place of work is pretty awesome!

At this time the school was also going through a period of extreme change and I found myself not enjoying the workplace as much as I used to. The new head was very different to the previous one and we clashed horribly. Our personalities were polar opposites which caused daily tensions. I didn't feel respected and my professional integrity was judged and questioned. I wasn't able to follow career opportunities that I wanted and the workplace was often not an enjoyable place to be. Living with such a heightened sense of anxiety at work resulted in a lot of extra stress and upset. Having the benefit of working for another organisation, Leeds Castle, opened my eyes to how staff are treated well. How they are valued for the skills they have, how thanks is shown in many ways and how to keep your staff happy. Things I was certainly not seeing at my other job in school.

This opened my eyes to the world of employee wellbeing and having cut my rhetorical business teeth in the world of network marketing I found myself with an idea. Nourish the Workplace was born!

By then I was deeply unhappy at work and it coincided with my youngest leaving primary school. It seemed like the perfect time to make a clean break, leave the school but to do what? Should I have a go at being a 'real' teacher? After being stung so badly with how I was treated at work, I didn't have the confidence that I could find a school I could be happy in, that would understand my family's increasing needs and that had a sensible enough workload for me to be present for both of my daughters when they had finished school for the day.

Teacher workload seemed to be at an all time high and morale looked to be at an all time low. So I took the plunge and decided what the education world needed was Nourish the Workplace, it was me who was going to make a difference to this profession. I took the summer off to heal from the traumas of the previous workplace and started in earnest in September of 2018.

The business has gone from strength to strength. I now work with schools all over the UK and Europe and absolutely love being my own boss! I fully intend to return to the classroom at some point, but not until I have made a lasting change to our wonderful profession and I know that I can lead a full and exciting life alongside teaching.

A constant throughout all this time has been helping people, not just through my paid jobs but also by volunteering. I am at my happiest when I am in the midst of an event with a clipboard and invariably wearing trainers so I can literally run around. I was heavily involved in the NCT as soon as my girls were born, running events and becoming the Chair. I then moved onto the school PTA, and loved organising the school fairs. My youngest daughter and I both belong to an artistic swimming club and I have gone from being a general volunteer to a fundraising member to now Chair of the committee. I am now also involved in Teacher5ADay which champions teacher wellbeing through Twitter and events such as PedagooHampshire and Teacher5ADayOnTour. I think some of my favourite and most rewarding moments though have been event organising, running around backstage at a dance show and organising PTA events. But add into that Drs and hospital appointments for 8 different conditions between them, battling with unsupportive education staff and a mental health service that is so broken you can't just leave them to help you. This all needs next level organisation and is more like a part time job.

Volunteering is a real test of your PA skills, you are giving your time and energy for free, on top of whatever job you hold and family commitments, and the only payback you get is the satisfaction that it goes well. The pressure can be immense, if it goes wrong the stakes are high. No money is raised, parents are upset, people are annoyed that their time was wasted, 5 year olds crying because they don't know where to go. But the buzz when it goes well is incredible. I don't do it for the thanks, or the glory. I do it because I love the feeling I get when it's successful and you know you have made a difference. One year we planned the whole PTA summer fair on a football theme, only for England to be knocked out in the group stages before the fair had taken place! But we laughed about it and still made a lot of money on the day! When you pop upstairs to the dressing rooms backstage at a dance show to see children having fun together while they wait, they have no nerves on the side of the stage and go home with beaming faces, you know you have done a great job at keeping everyone stress free with a well organised event.

The other PA role I have held is another unpaid one; being a mother to 2 children with special needs. There is an extortionate amount of admin to be done as a parent, keeping up with the emails coming home from school alone is ridiculous! I actually gave up volunteering for a few years as although it made me incredibly happy, I didn't have the time and energy I needed to make it work. I needed to concentrate on the mum role and also to put my mental health and wellbeing first. I felt like I was being pulled in 10 different directions and like I was juggling way too many things. Juggling with precious, fragile objects. I knew that sooner or later I was going to drop one of those precious objects and it couldn't be my family. I didn't have enough time to be everything to everyone and my family needed the best of my energies and time.

That's where my role in this book comes in, showing you how to protect and prioritise your mental health and wellbeing. Being a PA is all encompassing, it is often thankless and always hard work. You don't get the end of term chocolates from the parents or the praise in the local press and are often forgotten about within the staff as you are hidden away in an office. If you think back to how Jo started the book with the analogy of the Headliner, they are the ones that get the rapturous applause, not the manager, people often don't even know who they are. Because of all this you need to look after yourself. Your wellbeing needs to be top of that priority list you are always updating for others, so you can shine too.

We'll also look at how you can protect the wellbeing of the people you are working with, how you are so well placed to do that and what you can do to proactively help boost their mental and physical health, enjoyment and satisfaction of the job and their general happiness. That is as important as the results they get and how they perform at their job. It's a vital role of the PA which often gets either forgotten about or diminished. Not anymore!

Connect with me!

🅇 @nourishworkplce

ⓕ @nourishtheworkplace

⦿ @nourishyourinnerhappy

@nourishtheworkplace

🅻 @nourish.your.inner.happy

Kimberley Evans

🌐 www.nourishtheworkplace.com

🌐 www.nourishyourinnerhappy.com

4

How can a PA help a school as a whole?

Just like with the Headliners Manager, behind any great success there is a person or a team of people working towards that common goal. The role of a superhero PA is unique in that you really work alongside your Headteacher or Leadership team and these vary from school to school. However, holistically for a school, your ability to support your leader can ultimately affect the level of success they are afforded. Their job is to run the school, keeping the staff and students safe and happy while delivering education excellence. Your job is to assist them with this.

Starting out as a PA for the first time is exciting! If you are inheriting a previous PA's role, it would be sensible to try to have some kind of handover. If this isn't possible, arrange time with your leader about what they want. The big question is;

'How can I support you to be the best Headteacher you can be'?

There will of course be fundamental duties for you to fulfil but there will be other priorities that will be important to your leader.

My PA journey started when I had decided that now my children were both at secondary school, it was time for me to look for a new challenge on a Full Time, term time basis. I was already clerking for the governing boards at 2 schools and temping at a third school at the time. It was quite a balancing act alongside family life. A Headteacher's PA role was being advertised at a Secondary school in South Bristol, in 2021 for a September start.

In the usual way, I applied in the hope that I would get an interview and even allowed myself to wonder what it might be like to get the job (how long would the drive be, the hours, the pay etc). I was also nervous as this was the first 'proper' PA role I had ever applied for. I had done lots of other roles in the 20 years prior to this, all of which had lots of elements of working alongside someone and 'assisting' them, but never for a Headteacher. The closing date came and went and I hadn't heard anything, until an email popped up in my mailbox! Good Afternoon Mrs Deane, Thank you for your application for the vacancy of Headteachers PA, however ....

My heart sank - it was only at this point I truly realised how much I really wanted this post. Reading further into the email, the Human Resources department were actually saying that there wasn't enough interest in the vacancy and they were going to re advertise in September and would I still be interested in the post if they tried again?

What would you do?
At this point we were in the Summer term of 2021 and time was ticking on. Should I go back and say, yes please and thank you? Of course, this is what I did. What I wasn't prepared for was THE FEELING. The feeling that I shouldn't just wait and that my time is now. Call it gut instinct, or wind, I found myself calling the Human Resources department to basically say I think you're making a mistake.

My heart was pounding, and beginning to sweat a bit (I later realised this was part of the menopause but that's another story!), it was definitely squeaky bum time. Imposter syndrome started to niggle; Joanne what on earth are you doing! You'll sound like a jilted lover, or desperate! Too late, someone answered the phone so I was well and truly in it.

 I thought, OK, be yourself. You have strength and integrity.

After a little chat with the lovely lady in Human Resources, I had arranged for her to call me back when she had checked the situation with the Headteacher and the CEO. More phone calls later, and I had a phone appointment with the CEO's Executive Assistant to sound me out. Woohoo! This is what I wanted; a chance. If after this phone appointment she felt I wasn't right for the role, then that's ok. At least I will feel like I've had a fair shot at it. I had explained that I could be really good at this role, and if it doesn't work out then no-one has wasted any time.

The Executive Assistant offered me an interview with the Headteacher the following week - and I got the job. The Headteacher (we'll call him Headteacher number 1) said he was impressed by the way I had pretty much insisted that they give me a chance. I was over the moon. I felt like a superhero.

What did I learn? Trust the feeling. Whatever it is that's nagging at you in any scenario, you need to acknowledge it or at least take time to reflect and work out what isn't sitting right. Address it; it won't go away! Talk it over, write it down, sleep on it. Do whatever you need to do so you can look back and think 'No Regrets' (as quoted by a certain super friend). I also knew that this sort of challenge coming from a female may/may not be well received. I learned that being brave (even though I was sweating) could pay off. Now, I don't mean going in with arrogance or self righteousness, rather, being stoic enough to be my own champion and humble enough that if it didn't work, I would respectfully step away.

I was grateful to be offered an interview with a panel made up of the Headteacher, the School Business Manager, the Executive Assistant to the CEO and a representative from Human resources. The process went well and I was offered the role later that day. I was over the moon!

Getting to know your leader

 Getting to know your Headteacher will sometimes start with the recruitment process. This is either your own, or theirs. It may be that you are already in post and are recruiting for a new Headteacher (we will explore this further later on), or perhaps you are applying for the role of PA to an existing Headteacher.

 Research: My first Headteacher was also new to post (but already had successful headships under his belt). I set about doing research about him and getting to know him as a person as this would build the foundations of our working relationship. What would a good day look/feel like for him? How would he like to be interrupted during meetings? Also, lots of random questions, like 'if you went home and had nothing to do with a kitchen full of ingredients, what would you cook?' This 'getting to know you' part is essential to

any partnership, and even more so for you to listen to the answers. I'm a great believer in the ratio of 2 ears to 1 mouth. You'll learn so much about your leader if you actively listen and read their body language from the off - a secret superhero. Little anecdotes that they mention (such as these are my comfy shoes) will give you a layer of understanding of their personality that will be key to how best to communicate on a given day. Let me explain.

Comfy shoes? Well, when might a person wear comfy shoes? When they are relaxed or need to feel relaxed? Might this mean they are in a chilled out mood or that they are trying to help themselves feel chilled out by feeling comfy all day? Body language will help work out which it is and a glance at his diary might confirm it. Right, only a few appointments and he's got 3 hours of school duty today. This makes sense. At the end of the day, a simple 'how did the comfy shoes work out for you?' will spark further conversation about the effects of a small, seemingly insignificant revelation. Again, these little golden nuggets of information will help you form an internal dossier of what makes your leader tick. Be aware though, these shouldn't be judgements! Rather observations as you get to know them. They will most likely try to get to know you too!

 Anxiety about working with someone new?

This 'getting to know you' part can take quite a while depending on how open your leader is. They may be quite happy to reveal a lot about themselves (personally or professionally) or it may take time to get to know the finer details of their personality. It can't be rushed or pressurised. It's organic and natural, although there are things you can do to help things along.

As you get into the day-to-day mechanics of being a PA to your Headteacher, you'll both be presented with challenges and situations that require the utmost professionalism. Equally there will be moments where quiet humility is called for - trust the feeling. When it feels right, and you are in a safe space (more on 'safe space' later), one way to break the 'awkward' barrier is to take a leap of faith. You'll be putting yourself in the spotlight as such and revealing something personal or humble about yourself. Depending on your relationship, this could be a joke, a confession, or something entirely off subject. I remember once waiting for an interview for a role earlier in my career, and I was offered a glass of water. Without really auditing what was coming out of my mouth, I blurted out 'no thanks, better not as I'll only need a wee'! I could have curled up and disappeared into the chair! I felt the colour rise on my cheeks and more sweating started. Even though I felt it wasn't my finest interview comment, it actually broke the ice and ended up being a funny moment.

Depending on how receptive your Headteacher is to this will determine its effectiveness. For your relationship to work professionally, you will need to schedule in a minimum of 30 mins a week at 2 different points for catch ups. These may be structured with an agenda, or simple quick 'what's the state of play' conversation. Be an insistent superhero that these conversations take place for planning and for your own wellbeing too. I often say 'when we meet later, have a think about XYZ' to sow the seeds of what needs to be discussed. It could be next term's Leadership Meeting, next week's Governor meeting, dynamics of the leadership team, or smaller things.

There will come a moment when a little lighthearted fun is in order - you can facilitate this when you feel the moment is right. I like 'Quickfire Funny'. You essentially start a short off task conversation; What are you having for dinner tonight (food is always a great subject, everyone has to eat). Depending on the answer you can initiate a little fun 'would you rather' conversation. Curry or Pizza? Beer or Wine? Too hot or too cold? Star Wars or Star Trek? Book or Kindle? I could go on! Keep it light hearted and simple - unless you are feeling like the time is right for more poignant questions: English or Maths? Meat or Veggie? Labour or Tory?

The time you will REALLY get to know your leader is when they are under pressure. This may not always be a pleasant experience but it is inevitable. We'll explore this later in the book and especially the effect this can have on our own wellbeing.

What advice would you give to someone who is about to get a PA?

Be honest and establish a great working relationship!

Greg Morrison
Director of Secondary Education
The Priory Learning Trust

5

The basics of Wellbeing

Wellbeing is such a buzz word now, and that is wonderful. So many more people are protecting their health and happiness and learning how to use boundaries effectively. Mental health is being talked about far more openly and hidden disabilities are being given the recognition they deserve.

But what is often lost within all of this is what wellbeing actually is. And if we don't know what it is then we can't make it happen can we? In this chapter we'll look at what wellbeing is and how strongly connected it is to our places of work and who we work with. I'll explain some of the science behind it and break it down so you can easily identify how it will help you and others.

Is it as simple as being 'well'? But then what does that mean? The trouble is when you google wellbeing it gives you so many variations on a theme that it becomes overwhelming. If every website tells you something different you can't tell if you are doing it right or how to improve it. For a start we can't even agree on whether to spell it wellbeing or well-being!!

I've picked out a few that resonate with me; someone that has been working in this space for many years. I could write an entire book on this subject but I want to stay focussed on how it is going to help you and those you work with and for. But what is really important to point out is that wellbeing is very personal. What works for one, can be awful for another. And I think that is why there are so many different perspectives and definitions of it.

The Oxford dictionary definition is, "the state of being comfortable, healthy, or happy". I have a big problem with the 'or' in that sentence! I honestly think it should be an 'and'. What do you think? The Cambridge dictionary goes with a more rounded, "the state of feeling healthy and happy" which I think is much better. The American CDC explains the concept that "people perceive that their lives are going well", which I really like as it takes away the element of perfection. It is achievable and not overwhelming (CDC Archive, 2022). But I think my favourite comes from a research paper from the International Association of Applied Psychology (don't worry I'm not going to get too technical), "well-being is about lives going well. It is the combination of feeling good and functioning effectively" it then goes on to discuss that this doesn't need to be there all the time and that negative feelings are part of everyday life, but if your wellbeing needs are met then you can learn to manage them effectively. "The concept of functioning effectively (in a psychological sense) involves the development of one's potential, having some control over one's life, having a sense of purpose (e.g. working towards valued goals), and experiencing positive relationships" (Huppert, 2009)

I'm going to stop there with the definitions as that was only a quick research through the 1,470,000,000 results on a Google search! But can you see how this all fits into your role?

So moving on to how to achieve that. Again there are many different ways, but I am going to focus on two, Maslow's Hierarchy of Needs and the Five Ways to Wellbeing (Aked and Thompson, 2011) which are widely recognised as effective avenues to pursue and develop wellbeing. Don't worry, I'm not going to get too technical, completely the opposite, I'm going to break these down how they affect you, your job and the people you want to help.

Let's start with Maslow, as I think that can be the one people struggle to connect with most. It sounds really technical and academic, when you look it up it brings research papers and journals instead of accessible articles and the images have been over simplified so you are still left baffled.

The basic concept is breaking down the needs of humans into a hierarchy of importance. It also shows that it works by scaffolding; the needs higher up the pyramid are easier to achieve if the ones below are securely in place. It is a myth that the higher needs are unachieveable without the bottom rungs met, someone who is experiencing poverty can still feel a deep sense of belonging. But the stress of poverty may at times override that. (Mcleod, 2024)

When you look at how these 'rungs' are named; physiological, safety, love, esteem, and self-actualisation, it is hard to see how these fit into your setting, job role and responsibilities. But when you break them down it becomes more apparent. This is how I see how they fit into staff wellbeing in an education setting in a general sense. We'll come on to how to utilise these best for you and your headteacher in chapter 5.

Physiological - this can be seen as what we need to survive and although you may not think that is the responsibility of the work environment, when you see that it includes food and drink, sleep and going to the toilet (amongst other things) it is clear that our work environments and the working practices within them are most certainly responsible for some of this section. Having the time to eat and drink, remembering to do so, having the facilities to eat healthily, managing stress well enough to sleep well and having access to toilets all fall into workplace wellbeing. They are incredibly simple concepts yet the most forgotten about.

Safety - this isn't just about us feeling safe from crime, but from bullying, hate and discrimination. Feeling secure in employment and with your health too come into this section. When so much of wellbeing centres around happiness, it is easy to then see how these directly interlink with your state of wellbeing and how your job can affect that. Having policies in place for things like menopause and sexual discrimination comes into it, having an accurate job description and up to date contract too. A person's health doesn't immediately feel like it should be the responsibility of the employer, but think back to the previous section and how eating and drinking affects your health and it's time to think again. Add into the the ability to go for doctors appointments when necessary, being able to have the time to exercise to prevent health issues and the understanding of others when there is a problem all fits into this category.

Love - this is a tough one to get your head around in a work setting. When it is described as love and sexual intimacy then no, not directly. But when you remember that it is a hierarchy of needs and they rely on the lower rungs to happen, if a person is not having their physiological and safety needs met then they are not in a position to meet this need themselves. Going home exhausted from work, too tired to do anything else and being irritable with loved ones due to the stress at work can all have a massive effect on this tier. But there is much more to it than that. Belonging comes into this one, and workplaces can have a hugely positive effect on a person's sense of belonging. Working together on a common goal and making a difference to a community can be the positives. But it is also easy to lack in this area, especially for headteachers. It is a really isolating job and hard to find friends in the profession that you let yourself be real to.

Esteem - which leads nicely into this one. A misunderstood one until you realise it also means importance. Most of the things that come under this banner are quite easy to achieve once you get to headteacher or senior leadership, such as freedom, prestige, having the respect of others for example. But others such as confidence, achievement and self esteem are harder if things are not going well with your school. In education we take things very personally, we think of the school as 'our' school and when it takes a knock, leaders take that as a very personal failure. They will need help seeing their achievements so far and building up on difficult days. This section also has massive implications for your own wellbeing. Think back to Jo's analogy of the headliner's manager. You are an integral part of the successes of the school and the person you support, yet rarely get any of the glory. It is harder to map your accomplishments and gain the respect of others in your workplace, especially as you are often the messenger of bad news. So this needs to be high on your radar, to ensure your needs are met in this area. You hold a vital role within the school and others shine because of your hard work and dedication, you deserve the recognition and self confidence worthy of that.

Self actualisation - a very random word and sometimes confused with the previous tier, especially when it is explained as meeting one's full potential in life. But the important word to remember for this section is 'desire'. The desire to want the best for yourself, to want to strive to be at your best, It's living to your highest potential and truly believing that you are worth that. It doesn't go hand in hand with the previous tier, it is as a result of that tier being met that this takes place. It's being happy to push yourself further, to know your worth and make others respect that whilst inspiring others to be the best they can be too. Considering that last statement is a major part of yours and your headteacher's jobs, can you see how important the whole of Maslow's Hierarchy is? If you don't prioritise wellbeing, you literally can't do your job as well as you should be able to.

The Five Ways to Wellbeing have been identified as the practical ways in which you achieve more happiness and fulfilment in your life. I see Maslow's theories as what the workplace and employer can do to help an individual and the Five Ways to Wellbeing are how the individual can take responsibility for their own wellbeing.

Both should go hand in hand, an individual has the capacity to take responsibility for their own wellbeing because the workplace has created an environment and working practices that allow them to do that. The individual also should respect the workplace enough to look after themselves so they can do their very best within their current circumstances.

The five ways are; notice, connect, volunteer, exercise, learn. When written like that they seem really simple, I even saw them on the back of the bus last week. But we still find them hard to engage with, I think because we are simply too busy rushing through life and we also don't know how they will help.

So let's discuss each one and I'll show you how powerful they can be.

Notice - I think people find this the hardest to understand as it's seen as it's not very concrete. Notice what? What do I do when I have noticed something? I notice how messy the house is and how dusty my shelves are but then that just makes me stressed and anxious! How I see it is that it's about making a point of noticing the wonderful things in life, about slowing down enough to see things, to hear things that you normally wouldn't, then that puts a different spin on your day. This week I woke up to the sound of bird song for the first time this year. Instead of rolling over when my alarm went off with a groan of despair at the 6.20am start, I smiled and opened my curtains to see that the sun was coming up that bit earlier now it was late February and the birds were waking up at the same time as me. When you make it your mission to notice more good things in life you will find there isn't as much space in your head for the stress and anxiety or that you find that the smile you had over noticing how delicious your curry was at dinner gives you that boost of energy you need to get a task done.

Because these are feelings and not concrete things you may feel they wasted parts of your day, if you need help getting going then write them down. Note them in a journal, take a photo of them, post on social media about it. Although notice is the one I think people find the hardest to understand I think it's probably the one most people tweet about with the #teacher5aday hashtag. Sharing what they have noticed that day helps them identify with it and posting gives it validation - try it!

Connect. This can be connecting with yourself on a deeper level through meditation, therapy and supervision and connecting with other people. It's getting back into the habit of meeting friends in real life. The pandemic and lockdowns really affected that but so has social media. We think we know how a friend is because we keep in touch through social media, but liking their posts or commenting with a well done is not a proper connection. How long has it been since you have seen the people you call your closest friends or spoken to them on the phone? Connecting in this way is having proper conversations or bringing about real joy. It gives us a dopamine hit that nothing else can replicate. It can also be about making new connections, taking the time to say good morning to a neighbour or a proper thank you to the cleaner at work.

Volunteer - is the one people shy away from most! As I have detailed earlier in the book, I am a great believer in volunteering and at the moment tick this box by being the Chairperson of my artistic swimming club, helping Martyn Reah with #teacher5aday, and helping out with village events. But it doesn't have to be as big or as committed as this. Volunteering can be covered by offering to do someone's break duty, making a meal for a family in need or making other people a cuppa when you make yours. Maybe it's better described as helping others? But what's important is noticing (coming back to that original point) what positive effect it has on you and making time (I keep saying that too!) for it in your life.

Exercise - Probably the easiest one for many to engage with, but also the one most procrastinated! We all know we should exercise more but how do you fit it in? A quick Twitter search of the hashtag bought up beautiful photos of the Welsh countryside, Cornish beaches and the Swiss Alps. There were posts about 17km bike rides and 1o mile runs and gruelling gym sessions. That will either inspire you or put you right off! Imposter syndrome kicks in, you feel self conscious in your work out gear and decide to finish the box set with a cuppa instead! But please don't be put off, essentially you just need to move more than you are used to. These parts can so easily be linked to the other ways to wellbeing. Go for a walk and see what you notice. It doesn't have to be somewhere beautiful like the Kent countryside, your local town will still have interesting things to take your mind away from stress if you open your mind to it. Ask your colleagues or friends what exercise classes they would recommend and see how much fun can be had from getting involved in something new. Or delve into the world of online content and do a fun workout from the comfort of your own front room.

Learn - How have I got time to learn something new when I haven't got time to get all my work done? A common phrase! Why, when you are spinning so many plates would you make time to learn extra? Can your brain even cope with any extra information? But learning something new can help your wellbeing in many ways; raising your self esteem, improving your sense of purpose and giving you more confidence (NHS, 2022). It can be achieved in a wide variety of ways, many of which link with the other points above. Learning a new sport will be your exercise and could help you connect with others (I do this through my artistic swimming), learning a new craft will help you notice and learning a new language (through classes or online apps) will help you connect more with the wider world. This does come down to time, but when you think that when you are feeling better about yourself you are more productive you can see how it will benefit you in all areas of your life.

All of these 5 ways to wellbeing come down to giving the time to your own wellbeing. To recognising how important you as a person is and how prioritising your wellbeing benefits your entire life. You need to make the time for these things. Start small, a 10 minute walk with a colleague at lunch, making an extra cup of tea, learning a new word every day, Then when you see the benefits that is having, how much happier you are and how much better you are dealing with life's stresses it will be easier for you to devote more time to them and then, just imagine how transformed your life will be!

References

Aked, J. and Thompson, S. (2011). *Five Ways to Well-being: New applications, new ways of thinking.* [online] New Economics Foundation. Available at: https://neweconomics.org/2011/07/five-ways-well-new-applications-new-ways-thinking.

Huppert, F.A. (2009). Psychological Well-being: Evidence regarding Its Causes and Consequences. *Applied Psychology: Health and Well-Being*, 1(2), pp.137–164. doi:https://doi.org/10.1111/j.1758-0854.2009.01008.x.

Mcleod, S. (2024). Maslow's Hierarchy of Needs. *Simply Psychology.* [online] Available at: https://www.simplypsychology.org/maslow.html#:~:tex t=There%20are%20five%20levels%20in.

NHS (2022). *5 Steps to Mental Wellbeing.* [online] NHS. Available at: https://www.nhs.uk/mental-health/self-help/guides-to ols-and-activities/five-steps-to-mental-wellbeing/.

My PA is a member of the extended SLT, responsible for HR and Staff Wellbeing and supports with administration for VPs as well. I delegate meeting management and organisation, proofreading, initial HR meetings. There isn't a specific way we interact on a given day - we have regular and open communication as and when needed, in person. As we grow we have deliberately worked to find what works and what we need to avoid.

What advice would you give to someone who is about to get a PA?

Listen, be clear, honest and open. It is about being a team, and working together, supporting each other.

John Salberg
Principal at The Wren Secondary School
Part of the Excalibur Academies Trust

6

Be an Organisational Superhero Ninja!

The old adage works here - Fail to Plan, Plan to Fail! Place yourself in any important situation or event, there will be a broad and thorough web of plans and decisions that have got you to this point. Any type of organisational management is impossible to do unless you get time to think it through. This can be a very quick thinking process or something that takes a lot longer and reflection. In the main, knee-jerk or emotional decisions are unwise.

When you meet your Headteacher for the first time, or indeed at review time, you will each have ideas about how you would like to organise yourselves. It's important that you get to discuss this early on especially if as PA you are managing your Headteacher's email, calendar and phone calls. There is a huge level of trust here as you will be relied upon to be able to highlight situations and prioritise.

Expect the Unexpected

This seems obvious right? Life in general has a way of surprising us and sometimes in more ways than one at the same time. The best way to prepare for the unknown, is to at least get what you can control to a point where you're on your game at a given time. This way, when the unexpected comes along, at least the majority of your other responsibilities will already be taken care of or at least only need a little maintenance.

In the first 12 months of Headship, my Headteacher went through what can only be described as a

'Lifetime of Learning'. Even Heads with over 20 years service will not have had to deal with some of the real issues we faced during those first 12 months. I really hope you don't go through these issues yourself, however I'll go through them here (this list is not exhaustive). I could write an entire book about each of these, however hopefully the information below will provide you with a few ideas to start from and ways you could potentially get a few things in place in readiness if you possibly can:

Ofsted and Inspections	See Chapter 13
Death of a Monarch	The death of Queen Elizabeth - as a school, a Trust and a community, we observed the national period of mourning and avoided sending any correspondence home to parents and carers. Our school newsletter was extremely short and had a respectful picture of the Queen on the front in black and white. It's worth noting that although a Monarch is the head of the UK, not all

	members of staff, students or families will be of UK origin and may not observe the same values.
Death of a member of staff/school community	Unfortunately, serious one-off events can happen. As a PA your job here is to simply assist the Headteacher in supporting the school through a difficult time. There are various charities and Delegated Services who can help in such situations and when these things do happen, they will be very unique in nature. There's no hard and fast rule, however one thing to bear in mind which my Headteacher noted is paramount is to 'do no harm'. Even if you think what you're doing/saying is the right thing, the bereaved family must be involved in any communications or media. If the police are involved or there is a question over a possible suicide, please proceed with caution and take advice from the local Constabulary.
Fire in the school building	Hopefully your school will have an adequate tried and tested Fire Alarm procedure - there's nothing like the real thing to test the effectiveness of your plan. If you're not

	aware of the school's evacuation procedure, or have not seen it tested, then I strongly suggest you do so. A good time for a drill is in Term 2 when your newest students have had time to acquaint themselves with the school. Be mindful that an alarm could sound at any point in the day e.g. if the alarm went off during lunchtime or even before the first registration bell, what would the process be then?
Flood outside the school	As with any national or local crisis, communication is key. Be careful here not to under communicate. If the situation means the temporary and/or immediate closure of the school, all stakeholders must be notified clearly and concisely including the Local Authority. Deal with factual information (no hyperbole or personal assumptions). Be aware that parents and the local community could become anxious about a potential situation and possibly take to media platforms to air their concerns. Be as clear as you can to mitigate this. A school closure will also involve a preplanned or dynamic risk-assessment so all bases are covered.

	Just like with the COVID 19 pandemic, if the school is closed for longer than a few hours, students will need to have home learning set for them.
Industrial Action	Again, communication is key here and only deal with legal and factual information. If you are in a Trust you may be given a proforma letter to use, however you may be given licence to write your own. Be careful when setting home learning as part of the laws of Teacher strikes mean there should not be a requirement for striking teachers to set learning in their absence, or for the school to arrange cover. Seek legal advice if you're not sure.
Sudden resignations	This can happen on occasion and for many different reasons. Often, a member of staff who is resigning will seek a meeting with the Headteacher or simply give you an envelope to pass on to them. These situations are time critical and should be dealt with immediately. The Headteacher may want to call a meeting with the deputies to work out a plan.

New members of SLT	This is an exciting but busy time! It will be for your Headteacher and the members of the SLT to plan out an 'induction' of sorts and you can most definitely use your organisational skills to get this off the ground.
Student Permanent Exclusion	Permanently Excluding a student is always the last resort in dealing with one off or persistent incidents. There are very clear national guidelines on how and why a student could be permanently excluded and I urge you (or whoever oversees Behaviour) and your Headteacher to become acquainted with the most recent Government advice. Putting together an Exclusion Pack is very time consuming and must be done correctly (the case could go to a tribunal and the pack will need to be able to hold up under scrutiny). I suggest seeking advice from someone in your organisation or trust that has gone through this process before and make a clear plan of who will do what should the time come. On occasion, a Permanent Exclusion can come out of the blue (e.g. a serious one-off incident) or can

	be a combination of persistent breaches of the school's Behaviour policy. In this situation, you will need to demonstrate the student has been given every chance to be successful and any appropriate reasonable adjustments have been put in place.

School

Administrator

Only because

Full time multitasking
NINJA

Is not an actual job title

The PA Principles

Phone calls:

Depending on how happy your Headteacher is for you to manage their communications, I recommend never giving your Headteacher's direct phone number (or email) out to anyone, and likewise don't publish it on the school website. Your direct number should be given out to only the very essential people. Your PA email address can go on the website (as a contact for the Headteacher and/or as complaints handler). In many respects you are the gatekeeper for the Headteacher as this enables them to focus their time appropriately.

If your Headteacher has a 'desk' phone, I would recommend disabling the answerphone facility and redirect the calls to your own desk phone. In addition, keep an answerphone facility on your desk phone announcing it as the contact for both you and the Headteacher. Leave a message for the caller - here is an example (you may need to practise this a few times!)

'Thank you for calling XYZ school. You're through to the Headteacher
Ms Smith's Personal Assistant, Mx Ninja. If you would like to leave a message for either of us, please give your name, number and a brief description of your query and we will get back to you as soon as we can. Many thanks.

This will allow you to manage the calls and not leave your Headteacher with a constantly ringing phone which can become annoying and persistent!

In terms of sharing personal mobile numbers or Whatsapp details, this is purely down to your preference. If you can have a way to contact your Headteacher when there is no other option, then this may be a good idea. This could be something that evolves with time or perhaps happens quickly - the leap of faith can help you work out if your Headteacher would find this useful or, suggest some emergency contact protocols to start the conversation off.

Mailbox

In general, most PA's manage their Headteachers email, alongside their own emails and potentially the school main email contact plus any others that might be used! That's a lot of emails. You will get to know your most efficient way of working alongside your Headteacher and they may have their own personal systems they like to use. This is an ever evolving way of working as you go through transitions. As a start, agree with your Headteacher how you can identify for them the emails that need attention, which ones to be aware of and which ones I simply call 'traffic'. It's quite typical for leaders to get a little unsettled if their mailbox has upwards of 50 emails in it. If it's approaching 100 or more, then you need to address this as soon as you can.

Most email applications (Outlook, Google, iCloud) have a few systems already in place for you to easily mark up emails. You'll need to have a play with the settings on your particular application. G Suite for example has up to 10 mark ups for emails (like a 'star'). A simple system I use is below:

!	Important to do - URGENT
?	Someone is asking a question
i	To do - not urgent
✔	Read but no action required
>>	Note to self

Your Headteacher then, when they get to check their emails (sometimes for only a few minutes at a time!) can very quickly address the urgent items first. Be careful to make sure even if you read the email contents, that you remark the email as 'unread' so your Headteacher knows which ones they haven't seen. Likewise, you will be able to see all traffic in and out and there will be many times you will end up seeing information that is obviously personal and confidential. It MUST stay this way. These emails and the information contained in them are not for you to share unless you are directed that it is appropriate.

Calendar Management

This may well be one of the trickiest tetris games you'll play! I often liken my calendar view to Joseph and his Technicolour Dreamcoat! You will need to act as a filter for all requests for a meeting with the Headteacher. A new Headteacher will be like a celebrity in your school and community. Most members of staff and a good amount of parents will want to have 1-1 time with the Headteacher, and they often feel it is their entitlement. This may occur in other situations too, such as if a key member of staff is leaving, following an inspection, or if the school is undergoing any significant changes.

Obviously if your Headteacher requests for a meeting to be arranged, then it is a simple process of inviting the guests and booking an appropriately sized room.

If at all possible, try to get ahead of the requests. Looking at the First 100 Days book by Phil Denton, a timeline is suggested for a new Headteacher to be able to meet every single member of staff for a 10 minute minimum face to face chat with no agenda. While the book suggests getting this completed within the first 100 days, I found actually getting this done in term 1 is a good investment of time. If you can pre-empt individual requests from colleagues before they ask, you will have a smoother running term. An easy way to get this done quickly is to set up a spreadsheet of time slots in your Headteacher's calendar and share the spreadsheet with all those who you would like to offer a 10 mins slot to. They will essentially book themselves in at a time when they are available, which hopefully avoids colleagues having to book teaching cover. Leave a 5 minute gap between these appointments.

For unplanned appointments, you essentially need to try and ascertain why the person wants the appointment, when they want it and for how long.

Don't be frightened to ask the purpose of the meeting. If nothing else it will give your Headteacher a clue as to what to expect during the meeting. I will also help you work out whether the colleague should really be seeking time from someone else (their own Line Manager/Human Resources) or if indeed you are able to redirect them or even answer the question for them. The Headteacher is the highest paid individual in the school and each and every minute of their time is expensive and should be spent wisely. It is perfectly acceptable to book a meeting for the Headteacher for as little as 5 minutes. If more time is then needed then a longer meeting can be arranged with the Headteacher's agreement. Very few meetings need to be longer than 45 minutes and in general, this should be your 'go to' option as a maximum length.

Avoid where possible back-to-back meetings or those which straddle lunch time (unless lunch is provided!), early morning (pre 8am) or late in the day meetings (after 5pm) unless specifically agreed with the Headteacher. You will also need to be a timekeeper for your Headteacher. With their agreement, give a knock on the meeting room/office door or a 5 minute warning of when the meeting should be drawing to a close. Meetings should only be interrupted if absolutely essential. If a meeting is running past your usual end of day finish time, and you are comfortable to do so, you could pop your head around the door and say 'see you tomorrow', or if this isn't possible, a one line email or message will do. If this is a common occurrence, you can agree with your Headteacher that you'll tend to go without disturbing them.

Walk-ins

You will need to come to an unspoken agreement with your leader about visitors who turn up at the door unexpectedly. This will largely depend on the layout of your office in relation to the Headteacher's office. You could come up with a system that when the Headteacher door is open, it is metaphorically open for anyone to walk in at any time. Likewise with your office door. Whatever system you come up with, try to stick to it. The only exceptions are if the Designated

Safeguarding Lead for the school or Senior Leader requires to see the Head urgently or (as an example) the Trust CEO turns up.

Calendar Planning

There will be planned meetings of the Headteacher to attend regularly depending on the set up of the school and Trust. If you and your Headteacher are not colour blind, I suggest these non-negotiable meetings are one colour in the calendar. It will mean as you get used to the calendar system (most electronic calendar systems have the facility to use separate colours for entries), you can see at a glance where there are spots of availability and which events should be the last ones to be rescheduled.

I suggest you as PA have a minimum of two 30 minute slots per week with your Headteacher for catch ups preferably face to face or if you are in different locations, a video call can work. If you are working on a project together you will need more time than this. Again try not to reschedule this as when school life gets busy, your communications will be essential to the smooth running of the school, don't forget this is part of your superhero skills.

Once the essentials are scheduled in, you can start viewing your Headteacher calendar in terms of thinking, prepping and reading time. As an example, before your Headteacher has their appraisal, schedule in prepping time and try to ring fence this so it's protected. Similarly with Local Governing Body meetings and PTA meetings.

Professional reading is a good thing to try to schedule in, as is thinking time, (for you too!) however in all honesty, these are the first things to get rescheduled when something crops up! You can encourage your Headteacher to work offsite for a few hours to get focussed time as needed. CPD for your leader is also essential and so any external conferences where they can network with peers and learn new ideas in a different setting should be in the calendar too and logged as CPD.

Above all, your Headteacher will want to walk the school as much as possible and 'feel it'. Ideally this will be at various times of the school day, popping into lessons, supporting colleagues and being present during unstructured times. **Most Headteacher's will want to do this more than any other job on their list**, however in reality this is often very hard to squeeze in. The best thing you can do for your leader is help them stick to time, and get them out and about in their school.

You will also have your own workload to manage. Part of my responsibilities as PA is to be Complaints Manager, Suspensions Manager and gatekeeper for the school main inbox. It's important you are able to communicate with your leader about how you are managing your workload and how this impacts on your ability to strategically support them and your own wellbeing. You know how it goes, especially at the end of term when everyone is wrapping up their own workloads, yours will probably peak. If you can anticipate this coming, and possibly work this into your annual plans, at least it won't come as a surprise. It's also worth sending reminders to those colleagues who you rely on to send you timely updates that you require XYZ by a deadline to give you time to process what needs doing so you get to step away from your desk for the holidays with as much in hand as possible. That being said, your 'intray' will never be empty. You'll need to be able to allow certain things to go unfinished. Renegotiate times scales or check in with your Headteacher who can help you prioritise what can wait.

As PA, you need to be able to 'read the room'. This is a superhero skill that doesn't always come easily. You need to be able to look at your Headteacher's calendar, assess the morale of the school and students, the mood of your leader, the amount of emails and work to be done, personal issues etc and try to get a feel for what's going on. This is where you can really make a difference to your leader. To know when is the time to suggest a cup of tea, and allow some breathing space to regroup and focus. This might mean cancelling or postponing something, suggesting an impromptu walk of the school together, or simply shutting the door for a few hours. Some time to walk and talk is often a good way to reset and make sure you're both on the same page and realign yourselves. Remember you're both human beings and taking a 'moment' is allowed!

As a headteacher for over ten years I did have a PA. I simply couldn't have functioned effectively without a PA. I delegated the organisation of meetings, typing, filing, liaison with staff and a range of stakeholders. She also acted as a sounding board for my decision making and for providing advice. Also line-managed the staff in the main school office.

Describe how you interact/work with your PA on a typical day (if there is such a thing!)

We met every day to discuss our work for the day and then frequently throughout the day to catch up. A PA must have the correct skill set but also be personable. This is a very close relationship and so you must be able to get on with them.

Paul James
Education Coach and Consultant

7

Difficult conversations & safe spaces

We all know, sometimes in life we have to address certain things that we find difficult to put into words. For some, even the thought of it can bring on palpitations and the urge to run away. Lots of colleagues and friends may seek you out to confide in and for advice. It's common for even the highest level members of staff to come to the Headteacher's PA for a friendly superhero voice and use them as a barometer for what to do next. This is certainly part of my role I really enjoy as I can have a real positive impact on someone or a project. It's a privileged position of trust to be in when this happens and mustn't be taken for granted or misused,

 If you end up hearing information that is business critical, you may find you have a duty of care to your school and Headteacher to share this with whoever needs to know. Transparency is essential here and if something is raised with you, it's wise to check in with them as to whether you have their permission so advise the Headteacher (or whomever is the most appropriate). Sometimes, colleagues will purposefully tell you difficult information knowing you will end up telling the Headteacher (basically avoiding having a difficult conversation themselves). In this situation, it's a good idea to encourage them to speak to their line manager or the Headteacher themselves. If that is not possible, you may find you have no choice but to communicate and manage up to the Headteacher.

Be your
own
kind of
beautiful

— The PA Principles —

Other situations may arise where you have to deliver bad news to your Headteacher or even tell them something you are not happy about - remember, be your own superhero. As much as this type of conversation might make you feel physically sick (certainly does for me!) it's essential you are able to communicate this. Choose your moment, and be clear about what you need to say, and what you imagine the benefits would be for raising the issue. If it helps, I sometimes start with 'there is a situation' or 'awkward conversation coming up'. Be as brave as you can be - your Headteacher will value your message and respect you more for being straight with them. This also avoids tricky situations where your Headteacher may hear this message from a third party. They may query why you didn't bring this to their attention in the first place. You and your Headteacher need to be solid to enable this type of conversation to be dealt with professionally and for you to continue with your amazing partnership.

The concept of a 'safe space' will work in these scenarios; openly declare that your office and the Headteacher office are safe spaces where you (and anyone) can say whatever needs to be said with the protection of knowing there will be no judgements, just the best of intentions on all sides. When your job means a lot to you, at times you will feel overwhelmed and emotions may run high. Please try not to let this be a barrier to you doing what's necessary. I promise your partnership will be all the stronger for it.

 A good acronym for managing difficult conversations is noted in Leadership Matters book by Andy Buck. He describes conducting a difficult conversation as NEFIART. If you get preparation time and you know a subject needs to be brought to the table that you feel nervous about, you can use the NEFIART example to structure what is said to make sure you stay on track and cover everything you want to say. I've used this technique many times and have found it very helpful. Within the Senior Leadership Team, we will often practise this technique informally amongst ourselves.

We also use it well enough to be able to announce it should the time come. Eg: 'I need to have a NEFIART conversation with you. Let's get together for a few minutes?'

NEFIART

N   Name the issue (eg you took my doughnut)

E   Exemplify the issue (there was one left. It was mine. Now I have no   lunch)

F   Feelings (I felt let down as we had already discussed the doughnut)

I   Importance (It really matters to me that you know how important this is)

A   Accept (I accept my part, I could have been clearer in my communication)

R   Resolve (I know this can be resolved. I can be clearer next time and you could double check with me if the doughnut is for anyone)

T   Them (get their response)

The process of the NEFIART can be used in most situations, even if it is for a doughnut, or perhaps something more serious (e.g. the school gate had been left unlocked). The main concept is to remain calm, try to avoid interruptions and if you are interrupted, simply say that you haven't finished speaking and resay whichever of the NEFIART you got to.

It will feel undoubtedly uncomfortable however, all organisations and professional relationships rely on honesty and integrity (and conflict) to bring out the best. Ultimately, if any conversion will benefit your wellbeing or the students of the school then it is worth doing.

8

Supporting the wellbeing of your Headteacher

Much of what has been said in the previous chapters relates to your Headteacher as much as you. I think there are two ways in which I believe you will probably encounter issues with this part.

1   your headteacher not seeing the value of prioritising wellbeing

2   getting the balance right between the two of you

To solve this there needs to be a culture of wellbeing embedded in the school. It might be up to you to initiate this, educate others and shift people's thinking to begin with. But don't think that it is your job to carry that on indefinitely. Please reach out to me to discuss my view on who should lead on wellbeing within a school to give it longevity.

You may need to speak to other stakeholders such as Governors to help you initiate meaningful change. I am not suggesting going over your headteacher's head, but sometimes they are so busy they can't see the wood for the trees and need a helping hand. Other times it is actually the Governors or Trustees who are creating the culture that needs changing so addressing it with them makes sense. This might take some guts and gumption, but remember your superhero ninja skills and find a way to do it in a subtle and professional way.

Hopefully your headteacher will soon start to understand how valuable and empowering wellbeing is, how much it affects productivity and outcomes.

So how can you support your head in practical ways?

1   Diarise it

Just as I suggested to you to clear your diary for a lunch break, do the same for them. Clear 30 minutes at least of their diary and protect that. Make this the absolute last thing you rearrange or cancel and certainly don't swap out your lunch as a compromise. Ideally you BOTH need to have a lunch break every day so protect the time, and protect it aggressively!

2   Outside help

Supervision, coaching.

Work together to get to know your Headteacher's family and/or outside interests. You have to tread carefully here to ensure you keep professional boundaries, but if your headteacher's partner knows you are working hard for their best interests they will work with you on it. Encourage them to let you know if they need to be home early for a family commitment, if they have a doctor's appointment or a hobby they keep sidelining. As the keeper of their diary you have the power to make sure these things happen.

Encourage your Headteacher to lean on others in time of need. This will also help you and your wellbeing too. As much as you can lend a friendly ear to issues they may be having, offer supportive suggestions to work issues and be empathic with what is causing them stress, you need to understand your limitations. It can be too much if you are their only sounding board. You are great at your job, but there are others out there that are even better for certain situations. Supervision and coaching are incredibly powerful and can take your great work and super charge it. Research what is available to your leader and protect the time in the diary for it.

3   Organise it

As Jo has mentioned before, really getting to know your headteacher helps in so many ways. I would guess they forget to eat their lunch many times a week. They might forget important family dates (including anniversaries!). They might really want to play squash after work but keep forgetting to book a court until it is too late.

Assisting with all of these will improve their wellbeing, that will ripple out not just to you, but throughout the rest of the school. Find these details out. Have their favourite snacks on hand, know when to get food for them from the canteen so they eat and even organise gifts on their behalf.

4   Be strong

They may protest, or may even deliberately sabotage your plans for their self care. This doesn't mean they don't like you or are getting annoyed with you, it means they haven't understood the value of it, yet! So keep going. Remind yourself why you are doing this and remember the principle - Don't take it personally!

When it comes to assisting your Headteacher with personal issues, such as booking exercise classes or remembering important dates it may feel like this is overstepping boundaries. You have to do what works for you and what you are comfortable with. If you think the PA's role is to ensure the Headteacher works to the best of their abilities and one of your main roles is to facilitate this, personal situations can be a huge barrier to this. Addressing these issues can pave the way for them being in a better place physically and mentally and therefore being the best they can be at work.

What would I do without you?

This is often said in a very flippant way. Not because the person saying it doesn't appreciate you, but that they don't know the answer to their rhetorical question. They say it to show they understand how much you do for them and how thankful they are. But what would they do without you?

I'm not saying this necessarily in terms that you are going to leave, but more in terms of being off sick or having a family situation that you must attend to. I can hear you all saying now, "Call in sick? I'd never do that, I haven't got time to be sick!"

And that is exactly the problem, and even superheroes get sick.

You are so busy sorting everyone else out, looking after others and making sure they take a break, eat their lunch, go to the toilet etc. But are you doing that for yourself? Because if not, you WILL end up having to call in sick, if not for a physical health problem then a mental health issue.

You won't want to, but you'll be forced to. Burn out is a real thing and it happens to PAs too.

I can see you rolling your eyes as you read this, "Yeah, yeah, but when? When am I going to get the time to do that?" The answer is right under your nose, you need to prioritise your health and wellbeing as well as you do your leader. Actually, I'd go so far as to say yours needs to be higher. Yes, really! So you are then in a position to look after them. A great way of describing this is the Oxygen Mask analogy. You MUST apply your Oxygen mask first before you can help others. More on this in chapter 11.

You know how good you are at scheduling? At keeping a really tight ship of their diary? Well let's apply that practice to yours as well. Let's have a look at how to do that.

A small caveat, some of what is to follow has been said in previous chapters. I considered rewriting it, but decided to leave it in. Why? Because you need to hear it more than once to get it to sink in. These are hard things to change; ingrained habits that require a lot of effort to change. Chances are you only skim read the last chapter, so maybe a second read won't be so bad.

Lunch
You need to take at least 30 mins away from your work. Let me say that again for those who are skim

reading. Away from your work!!!! Eating your food whilst sitting at your desk reading emails is not a break. It doesn't count. If you can get to the staff room, that is the best option. Silence your notifications, take a walk to the staff room and see other people. This also encourages you to eat healthier. If you use the staff room facilities then you can keep food in the fridge, warm things up in the microwave, and make yourself a cuppa. (If these words are completely alien to you, then we need to have a chat, please let me help!) If that isn't possible for you, then maybe eat your lunch and then take a walk. You need a proper break from everything work related. If you are tied to your desk (again, please email me if this is the case) then find something to do to take your mind away from work for a bit. Watch something on your phone, listen to a podcast, read a magazine (be proactive enough to have some in the office). It's just really important that this isn't a working lunch. If you can manage more than 20 minutes then you definitely get a superhero gold star,

I'd love to see you all taking 45 minutes but I know I am pushing my luck with that number!

Breaks

At least once in the morning, and once in the afternoon (more if you are working later because of an event) you need to take a mini break away from work. Make a cuppa and go and find a colleague for a chat (and no, not work related, a personal chat), go for a quick walk outside, or read some more of that magazine.

How? Scheduling! Put these times in your diary, and in your head's so they know not to disturb you in these times, just as you do for them. Build a culture of respect for each other's wellbeing. Communicate with others as to why this is important and what you are doing, make sure they understand to only contact you in an emergency and respect that you are putting your needs first for a good reason. It will be hard not to be disturbed at all as emails will ping in and calls will still be made by others to you. So if you can't physically get away from your desk then switch off your computer. Yes, you heard me right. Be brave, you can do it! It probably needs a rest too and the IT department will thank you for it!

What is an emergency? Well that is a loaded question, but I would say the following are the only reasons your time (and their time when it comes to it) should be interrupted.

- Ofsted
- Safeguarding

That's it! Not "I really can't find that file" or "Can I quickly ask you to email xyz". They are not urgent and not emergencies. They can wait 20 minutes and when they are made to wait you are in a better place to deal with them in your best way, rather than hurriedly doing it whilst trying not to burn your tongue on your lunch, or spill yoghurt on your keyboard.

Your environment

I'm guessing you spend a great deal of time sitting at your computer. What is your chair like? Seriously, this is where you spend most of your day, your office chair should be perfect for you. What about your desk, or where your computer is? Your working day shouldn't result in a sore back or repetitive strain injury. These are preventable and count as your health and wellbeing. Do you have a blue light filter on your PC screen? These things need fulfilling to ensure you are well enough to do your job and your Head isn't left having to work out what to do without you!

Length of your day

It's very easy to let this run away with you and before long you are working a wrap around care day. It can be very tempting to feel like you need to be in before your Headteacher and not leave until after they have gone, thinking that it makes things easier that way. But this is unsustainable for your health and wellbeing, let alone way more than you are paid to do. If your systems are in place there is no need for you to be in before them. Everyone reading this will be different with different pay grades and hours specified in your contracts. I'm not encouraging you to 'work to rule' but to just protect your own wellbeing by not stretching yourself too far.

If you find yourself being needed at evening events such as meetings and open evenings then have a conversation about how this will impact your wellbeing. Time off in lieu is often offered but that means you are still working way longer in that particular week than is healthy and you probably don't end up taking that time that is owed you either! Taking a few hours off on the following day would be more beneficial to you, easier to organise and shows respect for your wellbeing and pay grade.

Having a life outside work

I really hope you didn't read that and think "what is that?". You are not your job, you have a job. I know it is very rewarding and you love it, but you cannot let it consume you. Boundaries are good. They are good for your ability to do the job to your best as people work better when they are fulfilled and empowered. But they are also good for you as a person. You deserve to be healthy and happy. If you are feeling like you don't have the time or energy for anything outside of work then there is a problem. Work should allow you to live your life fully, not the other way around. You need hobbies, interests, and time for people in your life.

But coming back to that statement "I don't know what I would do without you!", if the worst happened and you did have to have some time off. What would happen? I would much rather it didn't and putting the ideas above in place will help prevent that, but sometimes life throws us a curveball.

Could your systems run without you there?

If you are doing this role I would take a guess that you are a perfectionist and a control freak (I actually don't like the word freak in that title, it's way too negative, but that's a discussion for another time). Which probably means that you and only you know how to run your very well organised system.

As part of your commitment to your health and wellbeing that needs to change. You are far more likely to take a well needed day off to recover from an illness, or attend an important medical appointment if you know things are going to run smoothly without you there. Create a contingency instruction pack for yourself and for whoever picks up your most important operational jobs in your absence.

Here are some important things to share with a few trusted colleagues so that someone can step in and run the ship for a while if needed. It could be that another member of staff is drafted in to do your role for a while or your headteacher may need to access things themselves, so consider both options.

- Your computer log in (change regularly for security reasons, but keep others updated)
- How the diary works
- Where important files are kept
- How your head likes their cuppa!
- The non-negotiables/tasks that need to be done on a daily/weekly that only you do. There would

then need cross referenced 'how tos' for someone to know how to do them.
- Other small things that will make everyone's days run smoother if you know about them

Many schools run an effective system for class teacher supply, where there is a file in the classroom with important information about the class, advice on how to make the day run smoothly for that particular class, where to find the staffroom and expectations of the day. It is worth creating a similar document for your role, but as yours is a more isolated role than the rest of the school, do make sure you tell other people where this document is! I would suggest it not being on your computer or in your filing system as if you are the only one who knows how that works, then someone else won't be able to access it!

Having a document like this will give you the confidence to take time when you need it. Letting go of some of this information may seem hard at first, allowing someone to come in and do your job instead of you will be even harder. But if you can accept that it needs to happen it can be a really great example to set for everyone else around you.

No matter how you feel

Get up, dress up,
show up,

And never give up.

Anon

The PA Principles

9

Clerking

A lot of PA's are also Clerk to the (Local) Governing Board or Committee of their school. The role of a Clerk is very interesting and will expose you to a great deal of strategic conversation and the mechanics of serious high level operational events such as employee grievances, disciplinaries and student PEX's (Permanent Exclusions). The inner workings of any school are entirely different in each organisation, and the structure of the leadership teams will be different too. If you are PA to the Headteacher and a Clerk, you can join forces with your Chair of Governors and your Headteacher to make a really streamlined approach to how Full Governor Meetings are conducted. This will embed the foundations of school planning and strategically support your leader.

I've always been in two minds as to whether the clerk to the Governors role should sit with the heads PA as there could be a conflict of interests. Likewise if the School Business Manager is the Clerk. Either way, the clerk role (which is a separately paid role in many schools) is largely a silent one. You will be required to keep meetings on track if the conversation goes off course and advise on the timeliness of school policy reviews. Attending the meetings and minuting them is only a fraction of the work involved in being the clerk. The cyclical nature of Board and Committee meetings means there isn't a steady flow of work throughout a term, rather a build up over a 2 week period each time. This can make PA time management particularly tricky so you will need to set your Headteacher's expectations during this time,

A tool I have used to keep track of clerking in a school is the Governorhub portal. It is a paid resource by the school (however I believe it is excellent value for money) and will allow all the compliance work to be recorded, plus a secure portal to store all agendas, minutes and Governance documents. It is also the perfect place to keep school policies and a full schedule of the Policy timelines. All governors, the Headteacher, the Clerk and PA will have access to the Governorhub.

School policy is rather a beast to be controlled! Over the years, schools generally collect more and more policies, especially if a school joins an Academy as this will generate a whole new set. My advice is to keep on top of the planned due dates of policy reviews as they will creep up on you! A policy of any kind is there to protect the school and ultimately the Headteacher so it is imperative policies are kept up to date and relevant. You can really help your Headteacher (whether you are a clerk or not) by having a knowledge of school policy and when they are due for review. It is not your job to rewrite policies however an overarching knowledge is useful. Policies with particular importance are those which must be published on the school website - this is a Department for Education compliance requirement. In addition, policies that the Headteacher may use regularly should be close to hand if they need them e.g. Capability Policy, Behaviour Policy and Complaints Policy.

As PA and/or clerk you may find yourself involved in high level minute taking for important meetings where your notes will be used as evidence in a wider context. For example for a Suspension or Permanent Exclusion. Your school should have robust policies and procedures in place for these types of events that will help you and your Headteacher manage proceedings with Governors. It's a good idea to familiarise yourself with the grievances policy, the complaints policy and the Permanent Exclusion policy ahead of time as this will guide you should a case arise, This will provide your Headteacher with reliable support during times when stress levels may be heightened.

What do you most enjoy?

The feeling that I have contributed to something big, worthwhile and important. The challenge of something new every day whilst also coming across those things that I know and can now complete with ease, which I had never come across 12 months ago.

What advice would you give to someone starting new to a role like yours?

Be kind to yourself. Know that you'll never reach the end of your to do list. Reach out and ask for help - there's loads out there and you are most certainly not alone.

Kate Maynard
School Business Manager
Ashton Park School
Part of the Excalibur Academies Trust

10

Imposter Syndrome & When It's Tough

Imposter syndrome involves feelings of self-doubt and personal incompetence that persist despite your education, experience, and accomplishments. To offset these feelings, you might end up working harder and holding yourself to ever higher standards.

The term imposter syndrome is widely recognised and sometimes is too often used to describe feelings of insecurity or overthinking. Genuine imposter syndrome has been categorised by 5 separate headings by Dr Valerie Young, who is an expert on the subject:

The Perfectionist

Perfectionism and imposter syndrome often go hand-in-hand. Think about it: Perfectionists set excessively high goals for themselves, and when they fail to reach a goal, they experience major self-doubt and worry about measuring up. Whether they realise it or not, this group can also be control freaks, feeling like if they want something done right, they have to do it themselves. (I admit, I am definitely in this category!)

The Superwoman/man

Since people who experience this phenomenon are convinced they're fakes amongst successful colleagues, they often push themselves to work harder and harder to try to keep up. But this is just a false cover-up for their insecurities, and the work overload may harm not only their own mental health, but also their relationships with others.

The Natural Genius

Young says people with this competence type believe they need to be a natural "genius." As such, they judge their competence based ease and speed as opposed to their efforts. In other words, if they take a long time to master something, they feel shame. These types of imposters set their internal bar impossibly high, just like perfectionists. But natural genius types don't just judge themselves based on ridiculous expectations, they also judge themselves based on getting things right on the first try. When they're not able to do something quickly or fluently, their alarm sounds.

The Soloist

Sufferers who feel as though asking for help reveals their phoniness are what Young calls Soloists. It's OK to be independent, but not to the extent that you refuse assistance so that you can prove your worth.

The Expert

Experts measure their competence based on "what" and "how much" they know or can do. Believing they will never know enough, they fear being exposed as inexperienced or unknowledgeable.(Young, 2011)

 Many first time Headteacher's or indeed experienced ones will feel flashes of imposter syndrome creeping in at times. While this is perfectly normal, it can indicate the start of burn out so trying to spot it like a superhero can be advantageous to the way you support your Headteacher. Many leaders may not even realise the credible snippets of insecurity (and let's face it we all have times when work requires more of us than we think we can give), it does require a certain degree of caution. If your Headteacher is open about their feelings, it will be easy to be able to talk through the issues that are 'niggling' them. If you think your Headteacher may not be open to that kind of conversation, there are other avenues you can explore to help provide support. You can suggest a longer catch up where a thorough evaluation of workloads can be discussed and planned in. There will also be CPD training available for your Headteacher including coaching which could be a lighter way of suggesting it might be good to 'talk'.

Leaders who also have difficulty acknowledging their successes could also be described as suffering from imposter syndrome. Often no matter how many times good results come, they simply won't believe they are partly or fully responsible for it. Often in time, these successes will be reflected upon and personal recognition will come through.

It's tricky in these situations as often there will be little you can do to provide reassurance for your leader apart from being by their side as a silent superhero. For them to know you are standing shoulder to shoulder with them will go a little way for them to feel supported. Imposter syndrome is definitely a real thing and can be truly debilitating at its worst. However, I believe a small sprinkling of self doubt can serve a good purpose for someone in a position of leadership and power. It means those inner voices are providing a safety net against making irrational decisions and keeping the humbleness of a leader amongst their flock. Questioning decisions and reflecting on how things should be done will allow growth and experience for the future. Overthinking can take up a lot of 'brain space' however once you or your leader worked through the paths that overthinking gives you, the real picture of what route to take will become clearer.

When it's tough - When to stand up/when to stand back/when to stand in

The role of superhero PA to any leader is not always easy. The role of a Human Being isn't easy either! I'm assuming here that you'll probably have put yourself in a situation where you're saying 'yes' to more than you should and putting yourself under just enough personal and moral pressure to keep you in low range exhaustion most of the time. Sound familiar? Being emotionally invested is quite unavoidable, and I believe that level commitment will only work to your advantage. This of course in itself requires a big dollop of personal transparency. You'll need to know your own 'warning signs' and take heed of them. For me, my classic warning signs are missing gym classes (which I genuinely love), finding that I'm so tired on the weekend that I don't want to do anything except be totally lazy, eating unhealthily, missing chorus rehearsals, getting emotional plus many other things I'm sure my family can tell you! Being a superhero PA and a Good human being doesn't happen by accident. It requires a certain skill to spread yourself thinly and keep your head above water at the same time. Your leader will be having a similar balancing act to master. Most of the time, your professional relationship will be perfectly in tune where you can almost finish each other's sentences and each one of you will know when the other is having a tricky day. However, and inevitably, situations will arise that feel uncomfortable. Perhaps you've made an assumption, perhaps your leader has misjudged something, it could be a very small thing, it could be a huge thing! All completely natural when you work so closely with someone.

 So - how do you manage this?

 Workload

It's tangible, measurable and negotiable. If workload is becoming an issue, my first piece of advice is don't let it build up. Be honest with yourself and regularly review your short, medium and long term 'to do' list. It's a puzzle to complete but it will always be unfinished, pieces missing and extra pieces that you don't need too! Don't fight it, review it and speak to your Leader about how you can manage it together. You will be able to identify where the sticking points are, if there are any quick wins, items that can be delegated, cancelled or postponed. Don't keep it all to yourself, don't sit on it and let it stress you (I know this is easier said than done). I can assure you, your colleagues, your organisation and your Headteacher would not want you to struggle or suffer in any way.

Mental load

Intangible, unmeasurable, unnegotiable. If you're finding that the mental load is becoming overwhelming my advice is the same. I speak from experience! Tiredness, expectation and anticipation can build up and can easily unbalance you. Don't let it build up. Again, (and I can not emphasise this enough), be honest with yourself about what is causing this feeling, take notice of your warning signs. It might be that workload is partially responsible, in which case this is within your control to be able to review it. Make sure that you do! Be aware, sometimes (again from my own experience) if you have left it too long before reviewing the situation, you may find emotions might come to the surface. Please don't be embarrassed if this happens. It will feel awkward (no doubt) and crying (or worse is trying not to cry!) will feel misplaced but it is essential you let it out. Obviously try to avoid outbursts of anger and violence. If you think this could be a possibility, it might be an idea to get additional support either from your Human Resources Department or your GP

Personal load

Your personal life! If you feel comfortable to do so, sharing information about your home life with your closest trusted colleagues can be a safety net should times get difficult. It's the leap of faith again. It could be a big life changing thing like the death or illness of a family member, or something seemingly smaller with a big impact on your life e.g. your car is off the road, lost your house keys, family stresses. Your colleagues will be having their own set or personal issues, which they may share with you. A problem shared really is a problem halved, at least for a little while.

Your Headteacher will be managing their own set of stresses and pressures, and the more you can be aware of these, the better. Understanding as much as you can, and as much as they are willing to share will really support them. This does not mean to say you need to be a sponge and absorb all your Headteacher's woes - but simply a calm sounding board and a kind voice.

Stand up/stand back/stand in

I'll be honest; I've had to have a few tricky conversations over the years. Sometimes they have been instigated by me, sometimes instigated by someone else. As hard as it might feel, honesty is the best policy and the wellbeing of the school students should come first. Just as important is your own wellbeing, and harbouring any ill feeling on a daily basis will be torturous. Be as brave you can, choose your moment and get that niggle under control. You could pre-empt the conversation with a 'heads-up' first. Things to consider are what you want the outcome to be? What might be the best method of approaching your difficult conversation? A few openers are listed below, are all ones I've used. Once these words are uttered, you're in the conversation and actually getting things resolved is underway:

- Heads Up
  - Could we have a chat later - you're free at 10am?
  - All ok with you? Let's have a cuppa

- Openers
  - Ok, awkward/difficult conversation coming up…
  - We have a situation
  - I need to make you aware of something
  - I feel strongly about something I want you to be aware of
  - I'm really nervous, but I need to talk something through
  - I could probably have done XYZ differently,

The conversation that follows is your opportunity to say what you need to. Obviously there will be some back and forth - keep breathing and get to the end. You may hear feedback that is unexpected so be ready to be open to that (not necessarily to agree with it). Once a good dialogue is opened you are in control of how things pan out. Difficult conversations aren't called 'difficult' for nothing, however clearing the air, and doing the 'right thing' wins over the awkwardness in the long run.

- Closing
    - Shall we make a plan to get this sorted?
    - Thanks for your time on this, I really appreciate it
    - Next time, shall we…
    - I know this has been a little awkward - thank you for …
    - I'm glad we cleared the air

Whatever the outcome is, ultimately you want and need to be able to look back and have no regrets - and know you did the right thing at the time.

Be your own superhero.

References

Young, V. (2011). *The 5 Types of Impostor Syndrome*. [online] Impostor Syndrome Institute. Available at: https://impostorsyndrome.com/articles/5-types-of-impostors/ [Accessed 5 Sep. 2024].

What are the main things you delegate out to your PA?

Diary, liaising with staff, replying to parents, being my eyes and ears, helping maintain positivity in the tone and mood of the office, general admin and research.

Describe how you interact/work with your PA on a typical day (if there is such a thing!)

I see her first thing and we speak throughout the day as needed.

Do you enjoy/find it easy to have a PA? It took some getting used to. I answer my own emails and I'm a trained typist so I needed convincing that I needed a PA. I am now convinced! I enjoy having a PA and she is 100% trustworthy.

What do you find tricky about having a PA?

Remembering to delegate. Remembering that she doesn't know what it's in my head unless I take the time to tell her.

What advice would you give to someone who is about to get a PA?

Choose somebody who cares about people. The rest you can develop.

Headteacher

Anon

11

Wellbeing means you too!

 When I started working in the wellbeing area, it was very much teacher wellbeing. Support staff weren't only forgotten, but their wellbeing was compromised by the ideas implemented to support teachers. Thankfully there is much more of a shift away from that thinking and we are now pushing whole school wellbeing which includes ALL staff.

However there are decades worth of bad practice and bad habits to undo - at a school level and at a personal level. The very nature of your job means you are there to support others and that often means your needs are so far down the priority list that they are invisible to the naked eye. If you've jumped straight to this chapter (which would make me very happy to see you prioritising your wellbeing), I urge you to go back and read chapter 2 first. That will help you understand the concepts behind what is to follow and you are much more likely to implement them successfully.

You come first, work comes last.
That's a tough one to get your head round, but a necessary one. The wonderful Patrick Ottley-O'Connor is always saying 'put your oxygen mask on first'. He posts daily about how he prioritises his wellbeing on Twitter/X and although his title of 'wellbeing supermodel' is self proclaimed, no one on this earth

will argue with it! However I did question the oxygen mask scenario and we've had a giggle about it. When you think of the oxygen mask why do they say to put yours on first? It's so you are in a better position to help others. Help yourself before helping others. That I massively agree with. But unfortunately that then creates a culture of only doing it so you can help others.

"I'm doing this so I can help others put on their oxygen masks"
"I'm going to get physically fit so I can run around after the kids better"
"I should have a bath so I relaxed enough to deal with the stresses of tomorrow"
"I should eat a healthy lunch so I've got energy for my demanding job"

How about; instead of putting that oxygen mask on so you can help other people, put it on because you are worth saving yourself. You are worth it on every level. So do the things I'm suggesting not just because you want to be great at your job, a wonderful human, supportive partner and helpful friend. But do them for you. Because you are worth it. (Not a skincare commercial!)

Put you on the to-do list

I'm starting with this, the big elephant in the room, because if you can get your head in gear with this, the rest falls into place. Think about your to-do list. You probably have one for work, if not multiple and one for home things. Are you on that list? Thought not. I bet the happiness of others is there; buy a birthday present for your best friend, send thank you cards, and pick up your daughter from swimming. But is there anything on there for your happiness?

If you can do one thing for your wellbeing this week it is this, On your to-do lists put things for you. For the list at home I can suggest things like take a bath, have 30 minutes to read a book, see friends. For work, yes this applies to at work too, sit for 10 minutes with no work and drink your tea, talk to a colleague about non-work things, eat a healthy lunch, take a 10 minute walk outside.

If you are not putting yourself on the list, how are you going to remember to do it? Quite simply, you won't! How many times have you wanted to do things for yourself, to have go at prioritising your wellbeing, but then get to the end of the week and you didn't manage any of the things you wanted? That's because you didn't put it on your to-do list. That is what drives you. We schedule our days by our to-do list and if you are not on it yourself, it just won't happen. Self care and your mental health and wellbeing is vitally important, so rewrite that list!

And think about how that is making you view yourself. That you are not as important as everyone else. A lot of the issues we face as a society in this modern world are down to how we see ourselves and our ever decreasing self esteem. Anxiety, procrastination, self doubt all stem from low self esteem. And if you are never on a list, then you are not seeing yourself as important. Every day you look at that list multiple times, every day it tells you that you are not as important as everyone else. It's time to make the shift. Putting you on the to-do list helps you prioritise your wellbeing and does wonders for your mental health too. You are important!

Eat lunch

I'd like to add in healthy food, but let's start with the basics! Eat your lunch. How many times have you looked at the clock, seen it's already 2pm and then thought, "Oh there's no point in having lunch now, I'll just grab a biscuit and then have dinner when I get home." Would you want your children to do this? The pupils at your school? No! So treat yourself with the same respect - even superheroes need to eat. Your body needs fuel, it needs it to work well but it also needs it to survive. See chapter 8 if you want to prevent that happening!

Now if you can manage it, eat a healthy lunch. Your job is demanding, physically and mentally, and your body will use up a lot of fuel for that. You need lots of fruit and vegetables, proteins to keep you full and carbs to give you energy. If you are finding the afternoons a struggle, look at what you are eating, or not eating! You may struggle with this as your office is far from the staffroom and there are not the facilities close by, which leads me nicely onto …

Take regular breaks from your desk
Have your lunch away from your desk! Many people tell me they eat a sandwich or have a protein shake for lunch as they are easier to eat with one hand. NO!!!!! You shouldn't be working through your lunch.

If you need a professional's opinion on this, psychologist Dr Becky Spelman states, "By failing to take breaks, we run the risk of becoming run down and inefficient at work.". She goes on to suggest, "We all need to take breaks, and that we work more efficiently, making fewer mistakes, and having a more productive outcome, when we take the time we need to unwind" (Mirreh, 2021).

Make yourself a lunch that needs a knife and fork to help you take a break from your desk and have some time out. Or if you really want to have a sandwich or protein shake, at least have a proper break whilst you do!

Have hobbies

I can hear you saying to yourself , "Pah, if only I had the time!" and "I wish, when do I fit in time for that then?". The thing is you have to make time. Hobbies don't pay the bills, but neither does taking time off for illness, so take this as a sign that you need things in your life other than work and family. Hobbies boost wellbeing in so many ways, from exercising your body or your mind, to the dopamine hit from achieving something to the boost of knowing you are making a difference through volunteering.

I am a huge advocate for the #teacher5aday movement which champions the 5 pillars of wellbeing. Connect, Notice, Exercise, Learn and Volunteer. These are clinically proven ways to improve your wellbeing and mental health. How many does your hobby tick? Probably more than you think!

Knitting - notice and learn

Running - exercise, connect (if you run with others), notice (especially if you run outside)

Sports coaching - exercise, volunteer, connect, learn

Baking - notice, learn,

It is hard to initially find time to do these things (ideally schedule them and put them on your To-Do list, see above), but once you have made that effort and see the benefits it is bringing it is easy to carry on.

Have a social life

This sort of fits into above but it's so important I thought it deserved a mention of its own. You need human connection outside of work. Many people hear 'social life' and just think 'drinking in a pub on a Friday night' and that can be the complete opposite to what you feel like doing. Having a social life does not have to revolve around drinking alcohol or late nights. It simply means talking to other people that interest you.

Hobbies count as this. I do artistic swimming. It's a club sport, we have a chat in the changing room and laugh together in the pool. Going for a walk with a friend, or meeting them for a cuppa and cake in town, playing pool with friends, a game of golf even on a really cold day all count and help your wellbeing. If you are not up for physically meeting people, chatting to like minded people whilst you are gaming is great too.

How and why is this so important? You are way more than your job and you need to give space to that. Your job is very important, you make a huge difference to a lot of people, and the money that you earn is used for vital things for your family. But it is not the sum of you. It should be a part of you, but not your very existence. Seeing it like this helps you set boundaries so it doesn't consume you. Because when it does, it starts to negatively affect your mental and physical health.

Say 'No' - have effective boundaries

Which brings us nicely onto boundaries. These help you have time for the things mentioned above. Your role is all consuming, you are helping many people and lots of them have long or even random hours. But you are not paid to keep their hours or be there all of the time. Boundaries are hard because it is inherent in you to want to help and please people. You don't want to say no because that would cause *them* stress and upset, even though saying yes will cause *you* stress and upset. There seems to be a real fear in education to be able to say no to someone.

Boundaries are easier to set when you communicate why you are holding them. When we put whole staff wellbeing at the forefront of everything we do and start to really get to know our colleagues it is much easier to work to accommodate each other's needs and hold proper boundaries.

Yes, if you just say 'no' to a request, it may come across as rude, even said in the most polite way. But saying, "I can't do that meeting then as I leave at that time to collect my daughter, how about tomorrow at 8am instead?" is much better received. This also becomes easier when you put yourself on your to-do list as your self confidence and self esteem is healthier for you to be brave enough to do it.

Prioritise your health - mental and physical

With regular 'holidays' many of us within education enjoy, we get into the habit of putting off appointments until the school holidays. But sometimes that is leaving it too late. Routine appointments can certainly wait until then, as long as you actually do make the appointment. So many of us say we are going to schedule in the dentist and optician but then forget and then a whole year has gone by and you haven't done it. Sound familiar?

But more pressing matters need to be dealt with immediately, to stop them becoming more of a problem. If you get to the Dr at the first sign of a throat infection you will probably limit the effect it has on your work and get better a lot quicker. The same with mental health appointments. If you are seeing a counsellor or therapist, make that a priority as much as an important physical appointment. If you push it to one side and downgrade its importance, the negative effect that will have will be huge. That is avoidable.

All of these will probably need a significant change in how you operate, especially as your subconscious will divert back to prioritising others instead of yourself. Take it one step at a time, make small changes to your daily and weekly routines allowing yourself time to embed them properly before building on the great work you have done and you will get there. Just remember the mantra...

Wellbeing means you too.

References

Mirreh, M. (2021). *UK workers feel guilty taking a break, survey claims.* [online] The Independent. Available at: https://www.independent.co.uk/life-style/uk-workers-break-covid-lockdown-b1821051.html [Accessed 5 Sep. 2024].

12

Supporting an Outgoing Headteacher and Transitioning in a (brand) new Headteacher

 One of the biggest achievements in my career to date is my involvement in the recruitment and transition of a new Headteacher. If you find yourself at a point where you are supporting an outgoing Headteacher and a new incoming Headteacher, please be reassured that the stress involved at this weird time is purely temporary.

My first Headteacher and I had been working together very successfully for 6 months (he actually promoted me to Executive Assistant after 2 months) and he was making huge steps in bringing our school up to where it should be to give the best possible education for our students (after all, this is what it is ALL about). We were enjoying having an unspoken bond where a simple look could denote action.

I learned privately that my first Headteacher had an opportunity to lead at another school and this news sparked instant nausea for me, and the need for the loo. Obviously I kept this information to myself and did not tell a soul - it was not my information to share. He had been in post for 6 months and my mind went into a tornado of questions. I was stepping into that easy-to-fall-into-trap of trying to predict the future. Not even superheroes can do this!

The way a situation like this is handled will depend on how solid your relationship is with your Headteacher. Remember, they are still the 'boss' and more importantly a human being. A working relationship will survive anything as long as any given situation is dealt with professionalism and kindness.

 If you find yourself in this kind of situation, whether a colleague has been in post 5 minutes or for 50 years, it could have the potential to derail you if you work closely with them. It could be that your Headteacher is retiring, taking time out, moving on, or taking a promotion/secondment. For you, take a breath, step aside, do whatever you need to do to process this change. Go for a walk, clear your head or (as I like to) go and help out on lunch duty with a High Viz tabard. Ground yourself.

The weeks following the announcement that he was leaving were strange. I maintained professionalism and tried in my own way to make the situation as seamless as possible for him, after all we had a special connection and I wanted him to be happy. I will admit though, I was personally a little heartbroken.

There was a balancing act to maintain and as they say in showbiz - the show must go on. While holistically, my work and moral code is always to the students of our school, my loyalty was still with the Headteacher. Yes, I was in a tricky situation as my personal feelings could have easily spilled over - after all, my job revolves around an individual who is leaving. Where would that leave me? What if the next Headteacher wanted a different way of working? Or not want a PA at all? I honestly felt such a plethora of emotions at this time. I felt torn as to how I was 'supposed' to react. I was genuinely pleased for him as an individual, but also I was totally gutted that our school would face further instability. It also made me wonder was there more to his decision than what I was aware of? Did he not enjoy working with me? Was there a problem with the Trust? Did he think our school was unworkable? Was he being put under pressure from other sources? I'm pretty sure all these ponderings were simply just me trying to accept what was happening, and the likelihood is, he made a decision for himself without any other forces at work.

Once the news was finally 'out' and everyone in all the corners of our little world were told of the Headteacher's resignation, I was actually relieved. I'd known about this for a while and was glad it was out in the open. This didn't mean that I could go gossiping! Far from it. As superhero PA, the confidentiality and respect held for the Headteacher remained constant and even though colleagues, parents, and students were trying to get to grips with this forthcoming change, it was still NONE OF MY BUSINESS. How, when and why this happened was not my story to tell.

What came next challenged me in a way I could not have prepared for!

I am what I am

I am my own
special creation

— The PA Principles —

 Our Trust had to set about Headteacher recruitment. A long and potentially expensive process. If you are faced with this situation I would urge you to be as involved as you are allowed to be in this. You will ultimately be working side by side with the new Headteacher that is appointed, and even though you may not have a 'say' in the decision making, if you are allowed to be party to the process, it will aid your understanding for what type of individual will be your Headliner going forward.

 Reach out to the CEO or the Human Resources department of your school or Trust to let them know you would like to be involved, even if it is a very small part. Your wellbeing will thank you and also your CPD. The learning journey was huge for me in this process and I couldn't have imagined the benefits of being at the front line of making sure our school had our future secured.

 Now - don't be fooled! I can only say this now a good chunk of time has passed and fortunately our new

Headteacher is a rock solid superhero himself. It took a lot of extra hours and juggling to make sure our recruitment process was slick and that the two day interview ran smoothly. This is where you can really shine as a superhero PA - essentially, the project manager for the group of Governors and Trustees who are overseeing the appointment of the new Headteacher.

After the CEO et al had shortlisted, we were fortunate to have 4 viable candidates to invite for an interview. I found this exciting and nerve wracking in equal measure. I was to be in charge of logistically putting the interview days together. Each candidate had a chaperone to see them through all the tasks, and tests and make sure they got to where they needed to be at the right time.

My first trick: If you are able, try to stick yourself with the strongest 'on-paper' candidate. Be their chaperone for the day. Arrange for every person who has contact with each candidate to have a feedback form - the minute they walk through the door, they are in their interview. Get them to write down their feedback during these 'unstructured' times as often this is where candidates reveal their true selves.

Secondly: Power dress. Yes, it sounds cliche and very 80's but if you feel like a million dollars walking around your school (and essentially showing it off) you will shine like the sun. Wear a brightly coloured outfit so you can be seen (this little trick has worked for me many times). If people are lost or are not sure what is next, you need to be easily identifiable, like a superhero cape. Don't forget, the candidates are judging you too! Engage with them, ask open questions, and be respectful of the outgoing head. This is particularly important if any of the candidates are internal.

Thirdly: Try to enjoy it but be honest at all times. Overzealous comments or making promises you can't keep will not go down well. Be professional and no matter how things turn out, if you don't feel the candidate is 'right' then you must feed it back to the interview panel. Confidentiality is paramount here - a candidate's interview is personal to them and feedback or decisions made are not for general sharing. Even though almost everyone at school will be looking to find out little pieces of information about the candidates, you are not at liberty to divulge anything.

Our new Headteacher was offered the position at the end of the second day of interviews (May 2022) and then started the real work!

At this point a PA essentially has two Headteacher's to manage. Many PA's do this successfully day in and day out if they work in sister schools or in smaller academies where the Headteacher's are peers. However in a situation where one is replacing the other, there is a duty to the current Headteacher, but also a very real need to start building relationships with the new incoming Headteacher. This will take very careful 'passive management'.

Your wellbeing will undoubtedly be tested during this time, and you may find yourself wondering if you will 'click' in the same way with a new Leader, and how on earth will you re-do all the work you did with your current Headteacher!?

Like I said at the beginning of this chapter, this is temporary.

While you will be chomping at the bit to get cracking with your new Leader, there are a few things you must adhere to during this transition time.

 Your professionalism must remain constant throughout. Documents and information owned by your current Headteacher or the school and Trust can't be shared with your new Headteacher without permission. GDPR is there to protect you and the information your organisation holds. You will need to obtain a One Way Disclosure Agreement (a document your new Headteacher will sign promising not to share any information) for your organisation to have your new Headteacher to sign. Laptops and passwords are a must as soon as this is viable but be warned, there may be delays and restrictions on this depending on your school's protocols.

A new Head will have several legacy issues to address such as any ongoing disciplinary issues or long term sickness episodes. Even the most organised outgoing leader will most certainly leave some unresolved issues that the new Headteacher will need to sort out. This is entirely normal and to be expected. Again, discretion is important here however the only way your new Headteacher will be aware of these legacy issues is if someone tells them. This may be you or someone higher up in the organisation.

There are a few things you can do to help prepare yourself and your new Headteacher for this 'weird' time. There are a great many books out there for aspiring School Leaders however few explain this transition from a PA point of view. I read Dr Jill Berry - Making the Leap. This book covers the journey a

Deputy Head takes in their ambition to become a Headteacher and the ups and downs this involves. I found this very useful in understanding the personal journey my new Headteacher was undertaking. Knowing some of the challenges he would be facing aided me to refine the support I could give him (especially at a time when I still had a current PA job to do!) I know now on reflection this was time well spent and I still refer back to the lessons learned from the book. Another incredibly insightful book is First 100 Days of Headship by Phil Denton and Micky Mellon The premise of this book actually formed the basis of the new Headteacher's plan for his first 2 terms in post. We wrote the plan together and adapted it to suit his aspiring Headteacher ambitions.

What this gives a PA is a 'shadow' 100 day plan. Not everything can be accounted for (rather an understatement!) but it does make planning easier so you can pre-empt your Headteacher's requests before they become urgent.

The reality is your new Headteacher is going through a huge change in their personal and professional lives, and for a while, you are the only contact point with their new school. You may be imagining they are going to be the saviour of your school (and they most likely will be!) But so much change in a short time will be unnerving. They will be feeling vulnerable and excited all at once with a big dollop of Imposter Syndrome thrown in. They too are also fulfilling their obligations at their current school which will be a huge drain on them not forgetting family and personal commitments or life in general. A weekly or more frequent well being check works really well. This can be on the drive home from work (private) or at a planned get together at the approval of your current Headteacher.

My PA allows me to be a Headteacher. She manages the day-to-day work so I can concentrate on doing my job. This includes high quality admin and communications, but also offering strategic advice which I encourage. She has a 'voice' which is important to me and to the SLT. A great PA is all about the 'person' not the role, with kindness and experience.

Richard Uffendell
Headteacher at Ashton Park School and Sixth Form

13

Visitors, Inspections and Audits

Over the course of any academic year your school will have many visitors, potentially some Trust or External Auditors plus the chance of an inspection (either ad-hoc or 'anticipated'). These can include (but not limited to) Finance and Budget Audit, Safeguarding Audit, Pupil Premium Audit, Religious Schools Inspections, Ofsted, the Independent Schools

Inspectorate, ESTYN, Education and Training Inspectorate, Education Scotland, SEND audits plus any internal or privately commissioned inspections arranged by the Local Authority, the Trust or Headteacher themselves. If you're not familiar with which one (or more) of these applies to you and what they entail, please reach out to a knowledgeable person in your organisation who can help you make sense of it.

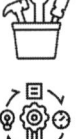

Preparing for an audit or inspection should be a matter of day-to-day work for most people in a school organisation and while as PA you won't necessarily be responsible for outcomes, there are lots of jobs to do that will immensely help your Headteacher and Senior Leadership Team in the run up to an audit or inspection, during, and afterward. Inspections and other audits are a moving entity and frameworks and definitions often (and do) change. With this in mind, it's important to note that while most of the information here will undoubtedly stand you in good stead going forward, please do check the relevant body who oversees the particular structure.

The themes to explore are what you can prepare in advance and what you can prepare once you are notified that the school will be inspected. That being said, the pressure of an inspection should not rule your life! There is so much more to school life than inspections. There are some non-negotiables, every day as a matter of course (such as Designated Safeguarding Leads ensuring school is fulfilling its safeguarding responsibilities, maintaining and auditing the Single Central Record, student safety). Some inspections will scrutinise Safeguarding and the Single Central Record as the very first thing they do. There must not be any gaps or mistakes here. Each and every adult who steps foot onto school site must be vetted (DBS checked) before they can be in school unaccompanied (all staff) OR they can be allowed to enter with a valid DBS check and credentials as a third party, OR they can enter school site but with constant supervision.

Regardless of auditors or inspectors, these rules are in place to protect the children. If they are not being followed without fail, the school is not functioning properly. And, quite rightly, inspectors can and will make less favourable decisions.

However, a higher inspection result should in theory be a bi-product of great leadership, teaching and support rather than an anticipated audit triggering a change in practice for the sake of more favourable decisions. The three I's are benchmarks that should be sought rather than ticking boxes for an inspection or audit.

Intent, Implementation and Impact.

If these three things are robustly in place with a proven journey of improvement, then an inspection result will reflect this.

The thought of a forthcoming audit or inspection shouldn't rule your Headteacher's life and rather than focussing only on this for a period of time won't be a healthy way to run a school. I recommend the subject of audits and inspections should be discussed at a senior level periodically (once a term) to be sure everyone is on the same page. Then, any action points can be confirmed and added at the next termly meeting. The idea being that should an inspection take place, the school is ready to provide the relevant evidence as needed. Please remember however, the primary goal for any school is to provide an excellent education for all in a safe and happy environment. Being prepared for an inspection shouldn't take away from this goal.

In Advance - weeks/months ahead of a possible full school inspection

Your Headteacher will have some kind of preparation plan in place for when an inspection takes place. This could be made up of a number of categories such as:

Personal Development
Quality of Education

Behaviour and Attitudes

Leadership & Management

Student Attendance

Nursery and Sixth Form (if you have one)

Early Years Provision

Special and Alternative Provisions

Overall Effectiveness.

There may also be provisions in place for 'areas for improvement from the last inspection'. If your school hasn't been inspected and is due, or your Headteacher is new to the school, make sure this is on their radar as a matter of importance.

The inspectors will need a fixed place to carry out their work in private and uninterrupted. If you have a good sized conference room this would be perfect. Depending on your school, you may need to dedicate a classroom or even the Headteacher's office for their use for the days of the inspection. Be available and visible especially if your school is big site/organisation

In advance of the call (and in addition to the work the Headteacher and Senior Leaders will be doing) you can organise yourself as gatekeeper. It will be your job when the time comes to make the days run as smoothly as possible. This means getting as much detail right as possible before the Inspectors even know they're coming to your school. Quick and easy planning to help get the ball rolling will really free up your thinking time and ultimately put you in a better place to support your Headteacher when the time comes. These things could be (but aren't limited to):

- 12 clean cups and spoons. Not your mum's best china, but a set that is reserved just for this purpose so you're not hunting around. You'll get through them pretty quickly and you don't want to waste time washing them up too often during the day
- 12 clean glasses and enough water to give a whale a new home
- Laminated reserved car parking signs - you'll need up to 6 of these. Don't wait to do this, the

last thing you want to be doing before they arrive is to try to find laminating pouches and a laminator. Advise the site team that bollards could be used and to have some on hand should they be needed.

- Extension leads x2. Your inspectors will thank you!
- 6 packs ready made up with useful documents enclosed. Make the packs big enough to add a lot of paperwork come the day, but in advance you need:
- Wifi Password
- Map of the school
- List of all staff with SLT, ECT's and Mentors clearly marked
- School day timetable
- Safeguarding Leaflet
- Fire Procedure Leaflet
- Spare paper
- An easy to read list of what you must do when the phone call comes. Depending on how big your school is, the phone call will arrive via the

main school phone number. You will need to brief the Front of House staff to know what to do (don't advertise to the whole staff body!) In most cases, the call will either be put through to you or straight to the Headteacher.

- Agree with your Headteacher, whether you should take the initial questions when the school is notified, or if they would like to. This part of the conversation is about 25 minutes, and covers basic questions e.g. how many pupils are on roll, full address, name of the Headteacher and Trust etc. They will also tell you exactly the days of the visit and the individual Inspectors names. If this person is not you, the School Business Manager could be an alternative. You will need to write down as much information as possible - stay calm and read back the information at the end of the call. Query anything you are not sure about at the time.
- Arrange for a termly 'Walk the school' for your Headteacher, School Business Manager and Premises Manager so they can identify areas

that can be improved or spruced up. This is useful not just for an inspection! A PA can provide a fresh pair of eyes on things that have just become 'wallpaper'.

- You will need to agree to a process of making sure the relevant people are contacted depending on the nature of the inspection, before word gets out into the community that an inspection is coming. Have their contact details written down - mobiles and email addresses - so you're not looking around for them. For a full educational inspection, this could include people such as (but are not limited to):
  - Any member of Senior Leadership Team who is not on site including the School Business Manager
  - CEO of your Trust and their PA
  - Chair of Governors and their Clerk
  - Chair of Trustees and their Clerk
  - COO of your Trust

The Day they Call for a Full Educational Inspection

Providing you have already done the aspects listed above, this will leave you free(er) to support your Headteacher and agree to your gatekeeper duties on the day the inspectors actually call. Ideally, there should be one point of contact for the inspectors and the rest of the school. This could be you, or the School Business Manager. As PA, your role is purely dependent on the needs of the Headteacher and therefore you can dedicate your attention to this without being pulled away. Be aware, it is not a walk in the park and you will have an active and full few days ahead. You will need to clear your Headteacher's calendar for the rest of the week ahead possibly a few days more) without causing alarm or letting anyone down. The process can be incredibly demanding physically and mentally so having fewer non-essential calendar commitments for your Headteacher could be a blessing! It also allows some mop-up time for the missed calendar bookings from the Inspection days.

Have a list of who will need to be assembled immediately. In the first instance after the very first call, the inspection admin will want to speak to the Headteacher. You can either (with the Headteacher agreement) put them straight through, OR agree a time for them to call you back on your direct line. This can be anything up to an hour later - this can work well if your Headteacher is not in their office, and the Leadership Team needs to be assembled.

When they call back, usually, you can be in the room along with the Designated Safeguarding Lead, the Headteacher and Deputy Heads. In this situation, you will be listening more keenly than the BFG and writing as much as you possibly can down about what is spoken and agreed. This conversation will take about 90 minutes. It is crucial to make a note of everything that is said. It is a long conversation that is highly intense. It can be easy for the Headteacher and the Leadership Team to miss something or forget exactly what was said. It's a bit like taking someone with you to an important doctor's appointment who can actively listen.

Once your Headteacher is happy the correct people have been informed they will need to notify the full staff body - the best way to do this is to hold an Extra Whole School Meeting at the end of the day for the Headteacher to verbally tell everyone. This should be short and to the point - your Headteacher will be like a celebrity! While it's tempting for staff to come to their Headteacher with immediate queries, in reality, the Headteacher needs to continue working on collating the information requested by the inspectors and the draft time-table of the day. Discreetly usher them out of the room as quickly as you can. Other members of the leadership team can field any questions and reassure the staff body on any anxieties. For a lot of school staff who have been in Education for over 10 years, an inspection will not be anything new. They can also support newer members of staff to navigate what is going on.

The general next steps are mostly dictated by the inspectors. Your Headteacher will receive emails with access to technology and a list of documents which they will need by 8am the following morning. You will also receive example letters to send to parents, governors and other stakeholders including students as required. These must go out promptly - especially as the letters to parents and students will have a vital questionnaire included (Parent View) which you need to encourage them to complete. Your Headteacher and Deputy will have to agree on the agenda of the day. The inspectors will give a shell timetable which will need to be completed as soon as possible. This is a big job so again, the Headteacher or Deputy needs to be able to concentrate on this fully. If there are enough resources available each inspector could have a chaperone to help guide them around the school, especially if it is a big site. They may not want to be chaperoned, so be ready to have them say they'd prefer to find their own way, or they may simply ask to be picked up at the end of their allocated activity. This may not be possible in smaller settings or Primary schools

 Your role in this part is to support your Headteacher and maintain your gatekeeper duties. As documents and folders are being collated, they will need to be vetted and uploaded. At the time of writing, only one person can upload at any time - I suggest this is you or your School Business Manager. This will take the pressure off of the Headteacher and allow them to be active in the planning process. A simple system where documents come to you by email (once they have been checked) and then you PDF each one and upload it will work perfectly. There will be many, many documents. You will need to name them so that you can easily pick them out if needed. Tick off the documents from the list given by the inspectors, so that nothing is missed.

Try to encourage only essential pieces of work to be carried out and when the SLT and Headteacher are satisfied all details are covered, everyone needs to go home. This should be as close to 'normal' finishing time as possible. I suggest that you don't leave anyone behind - agree a time that you must all leave the site and try to stick to it. As good a night's sleep as possible will set you all up for the next day. On the way home (or early the next day) stop off and get biscuits, fruits and vegan snacks for your visitors. Also plenty of milk, tea, coffee etc to keep you all going.

Inspection Days
An early start is preferable if you can manage it! Arrive at school with your supplies, comfy shoes and bright shirt or blazer ready to go - you need to be visible and available. Get to your office as early as you can, before anyone else gets there so you can get yourself straight and finish anything last minute. The Headteacher may call an SLT meeting before school, to have a cup of tea and create a positive mindset before the Inspectors arrival at 8am.

As PA you may be tasked with the 'meet and greet' of the inspectors. Usually they will arrive and meet in the car park and will enter the school together. Here, you can introduce yourself, that you're there to support them throughout the day, check their ID badges for Safeguarding and show them where the toilets are. Hand out their packs you've prepared. Remember - they're just people! They ultimately want exactly the same thing you and the whole school staff want: for each and every student to get a high quality education in a safe and happy environment. This is your opportunity to show off your school! The day will fly by. Your role will be mostly reactive and will hone in on your skills to preempt the requirements of the leadership team and the inspectors.

At the end of day, the Inspectors will leave at about 5pm, and no later than 6pm and will give you any requests to have ready for the next day. Your Headteacher will be given 'keep in touch' times with the inspectors as to how things are progressing and whether there are any red flags. The evening will be taken up by ensuring the information is ready, plus the possible generation of brand new documents that the

Headteacher may want you to prepare. You'll need to re-do the packs, tidy up, wash up. As a general guide, try to leave by your normal finish time as tomorrow (if the inspection goes into a second day) will be another early start.

Second Inspection Day

The Headteacher will probably want to meet the SLT at an early time - about 7.30am for a debrief of the coming day and any ideas they may have had overnight. Again, as PA it would be a good idea to get to school in advance of all this so you can get yourself grounded before everything starts again.

You can expect the inspectors to arrive at 8am - you'll be on a first name basis with them by now. Remember, some or all of them will have stayed at a local hotel or travelled a long distance to your school so a few tired eyes would not be unexpected. They may well have been working late into the evening so they are also prepared for the next day. The cup of tea you offer them will be greatly appreciated! Once you have settled them back into school, the work of the day will continue again. You will feel pretty busy, not least because the last 2 days will have been a whirlwind. Your Headteacher will have some more keeping in touch meetings with the inspectors throughout the day depending on how the inspection is progressing. Be mindful that as the afternoon approaches, pretty much everyone heavily involved with this process will be under immense pressure and will be feeling the effects of tiredness and adrenalin - including yourself! By around 4pm, the inspectors will have most likely finished their deliberations and will invite the Headteacher to attend a debrief of the whole inspection. I recommend the person who accompanies your Headteacher is able to type like the wind as this will be essential in trying to document the conversation. There will be a lot of information shared and you don't want to miss a thing.

The next step once this meeting is over, is the Inspectors will give another meeting to the Headteacher and any other relevant stakeholders, notifying them of the outcome. They are usually out of the building by 6pm.

My Reality
As you can imagine, the structure of the inspection days is simple enough. The right people need to be in the right places at the right time.

How the Inspection FEELS is quite another story! I've personally been part of 3 separate Ofsted inspections in 3 different educational settings. The one where I was the Secondary Headteacher PA was the most thorough, exhilarating and intense one out of the three. This is only my experience, and other experiences will definitely vary. The recommendations above are given after going through this process and build on the things I learned as a result.

When my first Headteacher was in post, as a school we were thinking about preparing for an inspection at any time. Our school hadn't been inspected since 2015, however in 2018 the school joined a Multi Academy

Trust which in theory starts the clock running again from zero. It meant 2022 was likely to be the year of our inspection. The Headteacher set about implementing a strategic step by step plan of our preparation and response. The document itself was a masterpiece down to the fine detail of what might be needed. It allowed us to try to anticipate what would be required so we could be as ready as possible when the time came. It was a great barometer of how we were faring in our preparation, while continuing to run a school and provide an education. The one thing to note with 'best laid plans' is that they must be kept up to date. A personnel change or framework requirements change for example, may affect your planning. Don't let this catch you out!

As time passed, my first Headteacher was replaced by my second Headteacher, and our Trust was in consultation to merge with another larger trust in the South. Our new Headteacher was savvy enough to know we were due to be inspected, especially as all the schools in our current trust had been inspected in the previous 4 school months. The Senior Leadership Team and the Headteacher put a lot of work into our plan alongside all the things a new Headteacher is trying to implement during their first 2 terms of Headship.

Then the phone rang - Monday 7th November 2022 - two months into our new Headteachers role.

It went like clockwork. The Front of School receptionist quietly and calmly put a call through to me in my PA office. 'Hi Jo, I've got Ofsted on the phone, can I put them through to you?'

Immediately, I began to sweat. I got my pen and a new page in my notepad and tried to concentrate on what was happening. At the same time, I was trying to attract the attention of my Headteacher who was in a meeting next door, without causing panic or oversharing this turn of events. I was able to stretch my phone far enough to swing my office door shut with my foot and stick my head around the door of the

Headteacher's office. One look at my face and he knew it was time.

While he wrapped up his meeting, I sat back down and grounded myself. I sorted out my desk, opened the window, and took a deep breath. Despite knowing what to do and preparing myself, I was still pink in the cheeks and had shaky hands. I was suddenly aware I needed the loo and that I MUST listen, concentrate and write legibly all at the same time. All this happened in a matter of seconds!

I spent the next 20 minutes or so answering questions from the Ofsted Admin person (who was lovely), then repeated everything I had written down to them so I could be clear on what was said. I agreed for the Lead Inspector to call back in exactly 1 hour for the first 90 minute call with the Headteacher, Senior Leaders and myself.

The Headteacher then rallied the troops, who again, took one look at our faces and knew immediately that our time had come. During this hour, I called all the nominated people on my list who needed to be told about our inspection. This task was quite nerve wracking! Calling the CEO, Chair of Trustees et al, and telling them this news was quite a responsibility and their reactions to it could vary considerably. I had to choose my words carefully and be clear and concise in my message. Likewise, I had to deliver the message, and get off the phone as soon as possible to call the next person, AND be ready for the call back in 1 hour. Squeaky Bum Time!

And so, we were off! We were given letters to circulate to parents, and a list of requirements. We arranged a quick whole school meeting at 3.30pm where the Headteacher addressed everyone to advise them we are being visited. By this time, it was no surprise as anyone in the building who was called to the Main Hall at 3.30pm with no information on why, correctly assumed it was to be told we were being inspected. This meeting was literally 10 minutes long and I managed to protect my Headteacher from queues of people, but also to have those critical conversations with staff who will have had an emotional reaction to this news. I needed for my Headteacher to have as much time as possible to start planning with minimal distractions. The school had many experienced leaders to turn to if they needed something urgent.

Then, back to our safe space, our offices and desks to get to work. I was feeling a mixture of excitement and nausea! I never feared an inspection, I knew it could feel like 'make or break' for a school but I always tried to see it as an opportunity. An opportunity for a school to shine, for colleagues to shine, for students to shine - and for a PA to shine. Try to see it as a chance to really get grips with the mechanics of your school and to liaise with members of the school team (as high up as CEO) that you would otherwise not spend a great deal of time with.

We set up a kind of virtual conveyor belt where I was gatekeeper to the Ofsted Portal. All documents went through me to be pdf'd and uploaded, and I ticked them off of the list as I went. My fingers were typing so fast! My rumbling tummy reminded me that the whole team who are staying on site to get this work done will be super hungry. Our amazing School Business Manager (who was actually at home very poorly on this particular day, but holds the pursestrings!) arranged for pizzas to be ordered for us to share as we just needed carbs. More and more carbs! I was so grateful to be given a couple of slices of oily cheesy pizza and pretty much inhaled it - it may have been the best pizza ever!

 Spare a thought for your Headteacher at this moment. Have they eaten? Had a drink? In most cases they will appear completely calm and focussed (our Headteacher was stoic!) however there is going to be a time where the reality of this situation starts to sink in. Be ready!

After a long evening, and as members of the team gradually went home, myself and my Headteacher finally left the building at 10pm. In hindsight, this was far too late however we made a conscious decision that this was acceptable to us both at the time. We had to make sure with our premises team that we weren't going to be locked in until the morning!

Day 1 arrived and I was in the local express supermarket at 6am getting provisions for the day. I made sure I had a bright pink blazer on, which I felt a little like a Pink Lady (those who know, will know!) and I whizzed around picking up what I needed. I was about half way around when I thought: 'I should have got a flipping trolley' and one of the shop staff shouted out 'Lady Deane - what are you doing up so early?'. It was a guy who I know who works at the shop who came to my rescue as I had bananas balanced on bottles of water and vegan biscuits tucked under my armpit! I was so thankful to have some help - this day has to start right! He helped me with all my stuff, and navigated the self-checkout (there is an unexpected item in the bagging area - my car keys!) He also carried my shopping out to my car too. He asked what on earth was going on. I simply said 'Ofsted are coming' in a semi-serious tone. What he said next was hilarious and kept me chuckling all the way to work; 'Don't they know who you are? You knock 'em dead girl!' I later wrote a lovely thank you message about my 10 minute dash to the shops that morning and by all accounts he received an award from his Manager as a result. Win:Win.

I got to work and settled in. I set up several kettles to keep hot drinks flowing and filled the fridge in my office with cold water and snacks. I also had paracetamol and lots more carbs to keep us going. No one had properly slept last night - the general consensus was that we were 'pumped up' for the day ahead. It's a good thing too because we needed the adrenalin to keep us going. The inspectors arrived and we were off - the right people were deposited in the right places at the right times. Perfect.

This moment of calm lasted about 5 minutes when the School Business Manager walked past my office in a rush. 'Jo - have you seen what is outside? There's a van!' All manner of thoughts ran through my head as I dashed up from my seat and joined her walking towards the school main entrance. Sure enough there was a white van with a 'message' painted on the side, parked across the school entrance doors. On closer inspection, we could see this was actually a protestor making their feelings clear about our SEN provision.

So, what to do?

The School Business Manager and I surveyed the situation from inside the building to start with. Do we know who this is? Are they dangerous? How many of them are there? As other colleagues were around and saw the van pull up, there were lots of theories on this unexpected event. Once we caught our breath and felt relatively comfortable with the situation we were in, the School Business Manager and I went out to try to get the 'man in the van' to move on. While the man was peaceful, non-aggressive, and polite, we were unable to convince him to leave.

I stepped away to think through what I needed to do. There were several people around who could keep watch and call the police. My job was to inform the CEO and the COO - and decide whether to tell the Headteacher (who was in lesson observations with the Lead Inspector!) The CEO and COO set about writing an in situ Risk Assessment and I wrote a timeline of events. To say my heart was thumping is an understatement! I knew this could throw us off balance and at this point I had no idea how this incident would come to an end. Would we have to lock-down the school? Were there going to be more protestors arriving? Would they still be present during the students' break time? What if suddenly the situation were to change? But, we were calm and purposeful and I knew we had the right support around us. I was then advised that the inspectors had been independently tipped off that there was a protest on site.

 I then had no choice.

With the CEO's approval, I had to find the Headteacher and tell him what was happening. I set off around the school to look in the places I thought he would be. I was delicately trying to look in classrooms trying not to disturb the students' learning or cause unnecessary alarm. At first, I couldn't find him. Shit. Then I heard a voice behind me 'Jo - ok? I saw a flash of pink go past the door'. Yes! My pink blazer came up trumps! I started with 'we have a situation', and the rest followed. Clear, calm and concise. Factual information. We had a small discussion about what to do, and agreed there was nothing additional to be done at this point, as the CEO had 'eyes' on the protester at all times.

All told, the van was on site for about 90 minutes. He didn't cause a fuss or cause any danger (although we could never be sure of this!) He was politely told by our Head of Premises that we had called the police and did he know his vehicle's MOT had expired? He was gone within 15 minutes.

This had all happened before 10.30am - crikey! Fortunately, the CEO was on site with me and we stood shoulder to shoulder as a mark of solidarity for the rest of the school. I'm so thankful he was there. A calm experienced leader who didn't rush in all guns blazing was exactly what we needed. No Drama.

The next few hours passed without incident. The inspectors kept to their timetable meticulously and I found this incredibly impressive. We were receiving bits of good feedback and generally the team felt positive about how the day was progressing. The Lead Inspector had a 'keeping in touch' brief with the Headteacher and gave guidance on what they would be looking for tomorrow when they returned.

 Once again, we returned to our safe spaces, our offices and desks. The room our inspectors were using was the Headteacher's office, and it needed a good tidy up. Our school doesn't have a conference room to house a meeting of this scale. We did a clean up and set to work on the additional requirements the inspectors wanted. Very similarly to the night before, we set up a system where all documents were vetted and uploaded. This time though we also printed off documents we wanted to show off to the inspectors and literally shove it under their noses! This was part of my job to do. Our School Business Manager popped out to get us all a 'chippy tea' and again we stuffed our faces with fried food, mushy peas (yum) and curry sauce (yuk). The only problem was that the food made the offices stink! We all agreed not to stay any later than 10pm and we pretty much stuck to it.

When I got home, I could barely speak (certainly a rare thing). Thankfully my family didn't expect too much from me and I crawled into bed. Didn't take my make-up off, didn't brush my teeth, did not pass Go, did not collect $200. I was asleep within seconds.

My alarm went off at 5am on day 2. I had managed 6 hours sleep - not too bad but certainly not sustainable. My wellbeing was being tested for sure. Little did I know this was going to be the least of our problems today. Our Senior Leadership Team Whatsapp group messages were alive with motivational memes and messages of positivity from everyone. Regardless of whatever outcome we were to receive today, as a team we had been bonded together in a way that we would remember for life.

Day 2 got underway and requirements were being ticked off one by one. Thankfully no protest today! The feeling was good and in general everyone was happy. Could we possibly allow ourselves to imagine that we would be graded 'good'? Was it within our grasp? I definitely had an angel and devil on my shoulders constantly bickering about what the outcome might be and why. It was almost too much to bear! Then, in a slow motion kind of Hollywood movie scene, the Lead inspector asked to meet the Headteacher unexpectedly. This could mean only one of 2 things. The inspectors have a duty of care to notify the Headteacher if the inspection is looking like it may be Outstanding (this was unlikely) or, if there is a risk that we could fall very short. I knew our school was not yet

Outstanding, and in my heart I thought we could achieve a Good rating. Our previous inspection in 2015 was Good but that was a lifetime and 5 headteachers ago and a different framework! If we landed on a less favourable decision then we would obviously have to accept it and work even harder to bring the standard up. But to imagine a scenario worse than this would be hard (not impossible) to bounce back from especially under a new Headteacher. None of this was his fault. We just needed to get through this as best we could.

This was not pleasant. A feeling of dread took over. The inspectors allowed the necessary people to try to identify the necessary evidence to prove we were a good school and what they thought they had uncovered was not systemic, rather an anomaly (which it was!) During this time, there was absolutely nothing we could do except let our colleagues do their jobs, and hope it would be enough to get us through to a positive outcome. I felt sick to my stomach. Not for myself, but for our school and the community. For the Headteacher (who had only officially been in post for

2 months), for all the staff and students who had endured so much instability for so long. I went to find the Headteacher. A man who I respect so fully, who had worked so hard in the short time he had been in post. I wanted to blurt out 'it's not fair!' and 'they haven't given you time' but it would not have helped. We sat in a side office in silence. I asked him only 2 questions: is there anything I could do? And, do you want to be on your own? He answered No to both. So, we just sat quietly, wishing and hoping for the best, but also preparing ourselves for the worst. We were quietly planning in our own minds, how to break any adverse news to the staff body and the wider community. How to try to not allow this to disrupt our flow of amazing work and aspirations. Knowing that truthfully, it could hurt. A lot.

I'm not sure how long we sat there, but we knew the time was approaching where the inspectors were beginning to start their deliberations. We stayed stoic. We started to get a few bits of feedback that the evidence gathered was enough to keep us out of a low outcome, and for now, that would be absolutely grand.

Then, before we could even catch our breath, the inspection was over and we could not provide any further evidence. The door was firmly shut and I was only allowed in to deliver tea and coffee. Time stood still for a while. There was a silence that took over. All the students had gone home for the day and colleagues were finishing up what would have been a 'normal' day for them. Eventually, the Headteacher and a Deputy were called in for the final debrief. All we could do was wait. As they walked in, I tried to catch the eye of the Headteacher but then realised I couldn't actually muster it.

The School Business Manager and I sat in my office, and tried to make idle chit chat to pass the time. Neither of us could concentrate on anything. An hour passed and I went to find the CEO and other deputies. I claimed I was checking in on them, but actually I just needed to see their faces. The CEO was arranging for the Trustees and Governors to meet the inspectors at 5.30pm for the debrief. The stage was set.

After what felt like an eternity, The Headteacher and Deputy emerged blank faced and went into the side room where some of the Senior Leadership Team had assembled. The School Business Manager and I followed silently as we squeezed into an office that should only have 2 people in it. There were 6 of us there! We looked at our Headteacher who simply said to his Deputy, 'You say it'.

We got Good in all areas. The little room erupted! There were tears and hugs and sighs of relief. There was disbelief and people holding their heads, mouths and knees. Was this real? I looked at the Headteacher in the face and shook his shoulders; this IS real! The hugs were tight and heartfelt, the joy that started to be allowed to be felt was emotional to say the least. We didn't have long to enjoy this moment: we were expected to meet the rest of the leadership team, Governors and Trustees in a separate room where the

Lead inspector would reveal the overall gradings to the whole team. We silently walked across the school to the designated classroom where they were all waiting, trying not to give the game away from our faces. Our colleagues who were waiting patiently looked incredibly anxious with anticipation.

The Lead Inspector went through the individual criteria one by one, reading off 5 Good gradings in a row.

As the smiles and relief spread around the room, the reality of what had happened only just started to creep into our hearts and minds. And then it was over. I escorted the Inspectors out of the building. Phew. They were gone and we were ok. Well, as ok as we could be; we had a pre booked open evening for KS4 families starting in 10 minutes. A quick dash to the loo, reapplication of lippy and I was back at front of school welcoming in parents.

There was plenty of adrenalin still pumping but tired eyes were a giveaway to the events of the last 3 days. We were all totally spent. The Headteacher and the Senior Leadership Team gave heartfelt presentations to the parents. It must have taken every bit of energy they had left to stand there and give professional talks. What legends!

Just as we had done the two nights previously, The Headteacher and I were the last ones to leave school at about 8pm. One last fist bump of triumph and off I went home.

As I walked through the door, I felt the emotion and tiredness finally hit me. I literally fell to my knees and cried. Big fat unapologetic tears dropped out of my eyes. It felt good to let it out. I could barely speak. My husband asked me if I was hungry. I genuinely didn't know! He helped me up and plonked a plate of food in front of me which I ate with one hand and fork as my other hand was holding my head up.

The next day was a normal working day, a Thursday. I got up at 6.30am; practically a lie in! The inspectors had advised that the result could be shared with the Leaders of the school. The Headteacher called a staff meeting at 8.30am to address everyone. He stood up in front of us all and started talking. His voice was slow, his body language was tired. A short speech praising our colleagues for stepping up and meeting our inspectors head on and despite some setbacks we could hold our heads high. It was a performance worthy of an Oscar! He had the room waiting on his every word. Then announced with a flourish and a click of the presentation slides 'we are a GOOD school'.

The hall was alive with joy. Lots of cheers, tears and 'whoops'. Clapping and hugs all around. It was magical. I'll never forget it.

Weeks later as term 2 rolled along and life carried on, we reminisced about our inspection and actually the toll it took on us who were at the front line of the whole thing. I wouldn't have NOT been there, but knowing now what a trauma it was on us all physically and mentally, I do wonder whether it was all worth it? The bottom line is the high quality education, safety and happiness of our students.

I learned so much from the process, and I know if and when we go through something like this again, it won't be in any way as traumatic. I'm sure I will pick up this book to guide me through my own advice!

What advice would you give to someone who is about to get a PA?

Be clear, be honest and be open.

Director Of Secondary Education
Anon

14

Tool Kits and Technology

What's in my toolbox

 Your toolkits, your armoury, your resources. Whatever you want to call it, it's important to have things that you know that work for you, to be there and ready for you when needed, but also as a matter of habit. in

Many people struggle with their wellbeing because they don't know where to start. We have come so far in the world of wellbeing in the last 10 years. But everywhere you turn someone new has bought out a podcast, launched a new app, written a book or started a new trend. It can be really overwhelming.

However, you just need to find your 'things', your zone or way to navigate this world. Just like I have a favourite spoon to stir the dinner with and Jo has her lucky Peace Lily, we also have certain things, which are tried and tested, that we know help and support our health and wellbeing.

The best way to work out what will work for you is to try things. But as I said above, that can be overwhelming. So I find the next best thing is to listen to others and what they recommend and try that first. Find people that are similar to you to ask. Maybe you can identify with Jo as your roles are similar, with me because we have the same hobbies, your colleague because you are local to them, or a family member because you have the same upbringing.

Asking people can be a powerful opener to nourishing and supportive conversations in the future too. Although we are getting better at prioritising our needs, we are not that open about it. But we should be! That way we can help others too. Sharing in the staffroom that you joined a dance group could help someone else find a new hobby, or posting on social media about a great new app that you have found could be the help a friend really needs.

Wellbeing should be in the CPD programme for every member of staff. One way of doing that is to share more about our own 'toolboxes'. At the start of staff meetings, or on a staff newsletter. I've recently seen a school set up optional sessions on a Monday morning for staff to lead a mini session on their hobby to inspire others.

An effective toolbox will contain different tools for different jobs. They will be varied to allow someone to do the jobs well. Your wellbeing toolbox needs to be the same. You need different and varied things to help support your mental health and wellbeing. What will work one day may be the last thing you want to do the following week. You need tools that will help you in different ways, things that nourish your soul, that heal your pains, that lift you up, that give you strength.

Running
Synchro
Crafting
TV
Walking
Chocolate
Meditation
Seeing friends
Eating healthy

I run, not as much as I used to due to perimenopause kicking my butt, but I run. It always amazes me that I can run! As a child I was never sporty. That's a lie, I was a great swimmer. But my family liked racket and ball sports. Tennis, badminton, golf, football. I was never any good at those. I was the child who stood as far back as a fielder in rounders so she could just chat to her friends. I tried to fit in and play tennis with my family as a teenager, but missed the ball almost every time. Then one day, I decided I wanted to learn how to run. Mainly because I knew everyone would think I was mad and wouldn't be able to and I do love proving people wrong! But also because it looked like a really satisfying thing to do. It gave me, and continues to give me, so much more than that. Yes, I have surprised everyone (including myself) by running a marathon not once, but twice. It has given me a release and space to think. When I run my mind is clear and focussed. I process everything that has happened to me recently and to me it is better than therapy. It helps me notice things, the birds chasing me, nature changing with the seasons, the cows in the fields looking up as I pass them which helps me appreciate the smaller things in life. I think a lot when I run, and that is good. Giving me time and space to think then helps my anxiety by not having those thoughts crop up when I am trying to sleep! It helps me in so many ways, I am eternally grateful that I started something I never thought I could do!

Chocolate brings me joy! I also bang on about healthy eating a lot so this may come as quite a surprise! But if you love something then take the time to enjoy it. Demonising it doesn't help, just learn to enjoy it instead of relying on it. My favourite is Dairy Milk, but I'm open to any kind really. Except Hershey's, no. Always no!

But sitting at the end of a long day and savouring a square from the wonderful purple wrapper is divine. I'm not going on any pretence that I only have one square, absolutely not! I frequently buy 1kg bars for a week! But learn to slow down and really enjoy it. And that comes from not demonising it. If it brings you joy, don't be embarrassed by it, don't hide it, or eat it quickly so no one sees. Value every moment. Be that lady in the Flake advert, embody that feeling!!

I never thought I'd be a person for meditation. I didn't think I could keep my mind still enough. Which is exactly why I needed meditation and you do too! The way I came about it is unconventional, but sometimes you need someone else to show you the way. I have my life insurance with a well known company that uses a sausage dog for its advertising. I get reward points for exercise (see running and walking paragraphs) but a few years ago I wasn't in as good of a habit with exercise as I am now. I needed to boost my points and doing a 10 minute meditation through a sponsored app got me the much needed points! At first I just had it on in the background when I was cooking dinner, but then I actually listened and took notice. What initially put me off was thinking it would take ages to do. I didn't think I had time for that (I know, I'm awful at listening to my own advice!). But the 10 minute sessions on the Calm app are amazing. I started putting it on my to-do list (see chapter 11) and found a time that I could do it every day. To start with it was after dinner as a transitional thing. Signalling the end of the 'working day' (as a mum, there is a feeling that you are not really done for the day till everyone is fed isn't there!) worked really well. But then I found myself falling asleep whilst doing it! At the same time I was struggling with getting to sleep due to anxiety, so I switched to doing it at bedtime. I can highly recommend doing this. Use headphones if you don't want to disturb your partner, but actually why not get them to do it too! I found that I rarely get to the end of the 'Daily Calm' that lasts 10 mins as having something else to focus on really relaxes me and helps me drift off to sleep no problem.

It has also helped me in so many other ways. Now I have learnt how to meditate. I can do it anywhere. At work in a stressful situation, having my bloods taken by a less than empathic nurse, when my kids are driving me potty! Deep breathing and taking your mind elsewhere can be done literally anywhere.

Walking is different in many ways to running. Yes, in the obvious way that it isn't as fast. But in the ways that I do it and how it helps. The pandemic was awful in so many ways, but I will always be grateful that it showed us how the simple pleasure of going for a walk can positively impact your life in so many ways. I did walk before 2020, but not nearly as much as now. What I do remember for BC (before Covid) was my husband's workplace having a walking challenge in January 2019. They encouraged everyone in the staff to join in and send in how far they had walked that day. They had league tables for different departments and a competition to see who could walk the furthest. What a wonderful idea! But at the end of January we stopped. I carried on walking on my own as I was working from home and needed to get out for some fresh air but it was mainly just me. In January 2020 we did it again as a way to get fit after Christmas. Again we stopped at the end of the month. During the pandemic, when it was the only thing we could do, we realised how much it helped us both. As with everyone else it was such a stressful time. Going out for a walk helped. It gave us time away from the news and work, time to talk to each other and the fresh air really helped immensely. The 'daily walk' is something we have kept going. With evening meetings and other commitments it is not always possible to do it daily, I don't want you to think I'm a saint! But we aim for at least 4 walks a week together as a couple or a family. How do we fit that in? 30 mins power walks around the village after dinner! Our longer walks at the weekend may be more scenic, but that half an hour after dinner helps so much. We talk about our day, off load, laugh, destress.

I walk with friends too. Exploring new places with a coffee shop and cake at the end of the journey is always fun and enticing. But so is our well trodden route around our local area, talking about our week, sharing funny anecdotes and confiding in a trusted friend about something on our mind.

Walking on my own is different, a whole different way of accessing self care. When I walk on my own I listen to audio books or podcasts. I work on myself, on my mindset. My well trodden path of 3 miles round the local area means I get 45 mins of time to work on myself, to listen to inspirational speakers, to be uplifted, to be inspired, to be told to go for it, to stop holding myself back. I get back to my desk and work smarter because of it. That time is golden.

Synchronised swimming is a bit niche and as much as I would love to recruit more people to the sport, that isn't my intention of this section, so just hear me out. It may help you find the thing that is missing in your life. I shouldn't even call it synchronised swimming anymore, it's now been officially renamed as artistic swimming but to me and thousands of people around the globe, it will always be referred to as synchro. I fell into it by accident. Not literally, I didn't actually fall into the pool! My youngest daughter had started 3 years previously, aged 8, we wanted to find a way for her to stay swimming without going into club swimming. She loved it, it was her life. It still is, aged 17! Her coach had some funding to run an adult course and asked me to come along to bump up the numbers. I said I would, but couldn't commit to coming every week as I had way too many other things going on. 7 years later and I'm still there, every week! What has kept me there is the team spirit, the joy of learning and the friends I have made along the way. And you can get that in so many other sports. Dancing, martial arts, football, netball and so many others. I love learning, as I have mentioned many times in this book. Learning a new sport can be frustrating at times, but fulfilling far more many times. The fun we have together, laughing at our mistakes, celebrating each other's achievements, and just being with other adults is such a boost to my wellbeing. Making myself go, at 8pm after a long, hard day can take some doing. But I never, ever regret it. It's a cliche, but so true. If you love water and swimming then do look up your nearest artistic swimming club, but I realise that won't be for many of you. But do think about what team sport you could try as it could be your missing puzzle piece!

Watching TV can often be seen as a negative thing. But I don't know why. If it brings you joy and helps you, then why should anything be bad? My husband and I have an unwritten rule that no matter what is happening in our lives, we come together by 8pm most nights to watch 2 hours of TV together. Yes, things like evening meetings, other hobbies and being a taxi to teenagers get in the way of it being every night, but we try to ring fence that time as important. We enjoy watching the same kind of show, either a crime drama where we can discuss the plot line or a comedy panel show where we can laugh about the same thing. It helps us to switch off and enjoy spending time together.

I also enjoy watching things apart too. I don't feel guilty for binge watching 4 episodes of American sitcoms on a Saturday afternoon. It makes me laugh, it's all good!

Seeing friends regularly is a must for me. Sometimes I have to really make myself make plans as after the pandemic and working for myself for so long I have become used to being on my own (currently writing this on a Saturday evening) but when I do make the effort, I never regret it. I fill my life with many different friends. I have my oldest (i.e. longest serving) friends from university that are my rock. We don't see each other very often thanks to our 7 teenagers having ridiculously busy schedules, but when we do we laugh till we cry and can't remember why we are laughing, and then laugh some more. I have friends from baby days that are wonderful to reconnect with after long periods apart and catch up. I have former colleagues who have become best friends that know me better than I know myself and are always there when I need them. I have friends that I have collected along the path of this journey through life that I sometimes forget how they came into my life but am eternally grateful that they are here. We have fun and adventures, smile, laugh and make memories together.

Make time in your life for other people. The right people lift you up and make it a better world to live in.

I have always crafted in some way. I think I actually started my journey into being an entrepreneur through crafting in my teens. I had learnt how to cross stitch and had extra threads, with friendship bracelets being all the rage, I taught myself how to make them (no idea how, this was before the internet was a thing!) and sold them to my friends for a fraction of the price in the shops! I took up cross stitch again at university, very un rock and roll but I enjoyed it and then discovered card making after I had my children. This progressed onto scrapbooking, for which I have cupboards worth of stuff and 15 years of memories to catch up on. Maybe I should stop writing books and get on with that! My crafts of choice at the moment are crochet, knitting and embroidery. I do flit around a lot as this comes into the 'learn' element of the 5 ways to wellbeing. I love learning new things. I taught myself how to crochet and knit by watching YouTube videos. I'm not very good but love creating something with my hands that can be of use to others. I have made decorations, face cloths, scarves, blankets and toys. 2 years ago I reconnected with my love of cross stitch through the more modern vogue of embroidery. I've made images and quotes to put in frames, sunglasses holders and my most treasures projects - personalised clothing for my girls. When your teenagers wear something you have custom made yourself, that is the highest wellbeing score you will ever feel!

Apart from the joy on other people's faces when you gift them something you have made, it helps my wellbeing by keeping me busy in the evening. The pull of phone and social media can get me even when I am watching something really good on the TV. I think it probably has to be award winning like Line of Duty to capture me enough to watch without doing something else. So to make me properly switch off and help me enjoy what I am watching without the distractions of social media or my own random and haywire thoughts, I craft whilst I am watching. It's just like a fiddle toy really, just one that produces something beautiful eventually!

Healthy eating is something that came into my life 8 years ago. I will caveat this with I am no saint. I am writing this with a glass of wine on one side of the keyboard and a bowl of crisps on the other. I live my life loosely by the rule of 80/20. I make healthy choices 80% of the time so the 20% of my choices don't ruin my physical and mental health. This started with me wanting to have better control over my IBS and has led to me learning that eating healthily can positively benefit your life in so many ways. It helps with my anxiety, with my ability to work at my best, to live an adventurous life without too many consequences and have some control over my menopause journey. None of those things are perfect, but I know they are greatly improved thanks to the daily choices that I make and habits that stick. I drink at least 2 litres of water a day, I eat a healthy breakfast (protein shake made with fruits and vegetables), lunch (salad or homemade soup) and a dinner made from fresh ingredients (I vary the proteins, carbs and veggies as much as I can). It might take me a bit longer than if I grabbed convenience food or made choices that weren't as healthy. But in the long run it gives me more time. I am able to live my life fully, to follow my dreams, go on adventures and spend time enjoying the things and people I love. Pretty powerful hey!

Using tech to help your wellbeing

The pandemic was awful in so many ways, but I do think one of the positives that it did bring us is dragging education into the 21st century in terms of using technology to help our time management, productivity and wellbeing. I had already been using Zoom for years by the time we got to 2020 and lockdown hit. I had been working with an American based network marketing company since 2015 and had weekly Zoom calls with my upline and team and accessed training virtually through Vimeo and similar apps. My business, Nourish the Workplace was designed to be a virtual company, I was doing it way before the pandemic made it famous! I didn't want to be travelling around the country visiting schools as my family needed me at home, so I designed the whole thing to run from my office at home.

But even I have learnt new skills and systems that have helped me work smarter, not harder and I am a staunch pen and paper girl!

How can tech help you wellbeing? By streamlining your systems and working practices you can not only free up time to help with your workload, take a decent lunch break and go home earlier. It can ease frustration and stress, leaving you happier and enjoying your job more!

So let's dive into some things that might help you further.

Making proper use of Teams/Microsoft/Google features

I'm not going into specifics as it will date very quickly, new features are released all the time! But take the time to upskill yourself on the technology that is freely available to you. Lockdown and remote working has been great at showcasing what is possible now in terms of technology but I would guess that even the most tech savvy of you are not utilising every feature to its best. It's a great topic for CPD and shared learning within a school, get together with others and ask them for their top tips and share yours. Subscribe to newsletters from these companies, or their YouTube channels where a huge amount of free support is available.

Learning a new way of doing something is not a waste of your time if it will save you time in the future.

Asana/Trello

These are workplace management tools that help when multiple people are working on a task or project together or if you want to keep track of your own progress through a lengthy task. They help you break down tasks into different steps for you to take or for you to assign to others.

I like that you can assign deadlines to tasks and it will send you a notification that the deadline is approaching. As I'm still very much a paper and pen girl at heart I also really like the physical aspect of moving the task from pending, to working on to done. That gives me almost the same dopamine hit as crossing off something from my to -do list!

One of my pet hates is constant emails that could be discussions or conversation and apps like this help bridge that gap. Being able to comment on a workflow keeps the messages within the app (you can set the notifications up how you want) and doesn't flood my inbox. I'm a big fan of GoogleDocs and how you can comment on something others are working on and keep the conversation within that document. This is similar.

Google Forms

This has so many capabilities that I will not be able to cover them in this chapter. If you are reading this and can add any suggestions, please message either of us and we will share it on Twitter so others can benefit. But I can see this working very well when you need to gather other people's opinions or choices about something. From menu choices for a staff social that you are organising, survey staff on their opinion of a proposal. You can use it for staff surveys too, but obviously I'm not going to recommend that as I'd be putting myself out of a job! Again it's another way of keeping your inbox clear of clutter and avoiding the dreaded reply all!

Scheduling

This is useful in two different ways - blocking out time in an online diary and scheduling posts and emails.

Many of you will have responsibility for the school's social media posts, scheduling these can free up your time and your headspace. Meta (Facebook and Instagram) has recently massively improved its 'Business Suite' where you can schedule for both Facebook and Instagram at the same time. LinkedIn and X/Twitter have the capability to schedule directly within its platform (sometimes only on a desktop though, not the app).

Scheduling your time in the diary is nothing new and not 'techy' as I'm sure many of you will be very used to blocking out time in a diary for you or your Headteacher. But using technology to do this can make life a lot easier. We have already discussed the power of sharing diaries but using the online diary to schedule time to work on a task or project is very useful. When a new task comes in, schedule time in the future to work on it, put specific times in the diary so it gets actioned instead of forgotten about. If you are struggling to find time with your headteacher to discuss something, schedule in conversation time. And as I have mentioned before, schedule in your breaks!

Reminders

The above then gets even more powerful by setting reminders through an online calendar. When you assign yourself or your Headteacher (or anyone for that matter) you can set a reminder. But explore within your settings to set that for times that are best and most effective for you. For instance the default on Google Calendar is a reminder 30 mins before the 'event'. Sometimes that is too short a time and I need a reminder earlier in the day, for some tasks that are too far ahead and then within that 30 mins something else has come up, I get distracted and forget again! Find a system that works for you and your Headteacher to maximise efficiency.

Two screens

This can be a game changer in a really simple way. Although some of you will have adopted this way of working ages ago, I know many of you are still using one screen with multiple tabs. Having a second screen allows you to have a different set of tabs open on different screens and you can also drag and drop between the two. You could have your calendar open all the time on one and your day to day working tabs on another. During virtual meetings you can then have another screen with important information on so you don't have to minimise the speaker. Play around with how you have yours set up so that it works for you.

Sway for newsletters

Communication is a vital component to protecting everyone's wellbeing so we all know that newsletters are a great way of getting information out to parents and staff. Long gone are the paper kind that took ages to print off and send out, but digital solutions can cause stress in the creation and not be accessed easily when sent out so communication is lost. Sway is a Microsoft app so it is easy to use for most people. Newsletters can be created with it collaboratively meaning you can set a template, send the link out to others and then send it back with their content. This can be used for whole school newsletters to parents and staff newsletter to keep them up to date without the need for briefings.

Dictate function on Word/Google Docs

I've only just discovered this and whilst it was a lightbulb moment for me, you may be reading this thinking - well of course I use that! But I'll explain for anyone living in the dark like me! The dictate function on Word does exactly what you would think it would do, it's sitting in plain site on your top toolbar on Word and looks like a podcaster's microphone. Ensure that you have a microphone enabled on your device and then just say what you want it to type. Brilliant for typing up notes you have handwritten or multitask like a pro by composing a document with your voice whilst you are busy doing something else, like making a cup of tea!

It also has a transcribe function so you can do the reverse too, let it read aloud a document whilst you are photocopying.

Canva

Another visual creation tool that is just starting to break into education. I have used this website for years to help with visual content for social media. But it is also really great for making presentations such as

PowerPoint and documents more engaging and user friendly. The time your Head has for tasks is valuable and they need to ensure that the time they put it in is received by the end user getting the most out of it.

AI

Well how shall we dive into this one as I'm sure it will be divisive. I'm sure everyone by now knows what AI (Artificial Intelligence) is in terms of productivity, but how can it help you? Well instead of putting something into a search engine and then reading through the various (probably millions) of websites to then get an answer or solution, AI does all of that for you. It reads the possible outcomes and collates them into a 'perfect' answer. This can help you with research but also with creating. Next time you need to write a policy or draft a letter, use one of the many AI apps and see what time it can save you. You will always have to read it and tweak it to your audience, but boy does it save you time! Good places to start are Chat GPT, Gemini and Grammarly. Otter Ai and Fireflies transcribe meeting notes for you, from virtual meetings or have it running during in person meetings. You may feel that some of these apps are going to replace you, and the talents that you have. But we all need to evolve and embrace new ways of working, don't see them as a negative. Instead see them as a way to supercharge your powers even further.

The trouble and beauty of tech is that it is ever evolving. We're writing this is 2023/24 and at the time of writing, the above is relevant. By the time the book is published something better may well have come along and some of the above may have become obsolete. But the main message I want to get across is to be open to new ways of working and learning about new technology. It can be daunting, I totally understand that, especially if you are not the most tech savvy person. But ask those around you to help and listen to what they use; your IT department, other staff members, friends and family, even the pupils! Learning is good for your wellbeing!

Glossary

ADD	Attention Deficit Disorder
ADHD	Attention Deficit Hyperactivity Disorder
AHT	Assistant Headteacher
ASD	Autism Spectrum Disorder
CEO	Chief Executive Officer
COO	Chief Operations Officer
CPD	Continued Professional Development
DBS	Disclosure and Barring Service
DHT	Deputy Headteacher
DLD	Developmental Language Disorder
DSL	Designated Safeguarding Lead
EA	Executive Assistant
EHT	Executive Headteacher
GDPR	General Data Protection Regulation
HLTA	Higher Level Teaching Assistant
HMI	His Majesty's Inspector
HR	Human Resources
HT	Headteacher

IBS	Irritable Bowel Syndrome
EYFS	Early Years Foundation Stage
KS 1/2	Key Stage 1 or 2 (Key Stage 1 is primary years 1-2, Key Stage 2 is 3-6)
KS3/4/5	Key Stage 3 or 4 (Key stage 3 is secondary years 7, 8 and 9. Key Stage 4 is Secondary years 10 and 11. Key Stage 5 is student aged Post 16)
LA	Local Authority
LEA	Local Education Authority
LSA	Learning Support Assistant
PA	Personal Assistant
PEX	Permanent Exclusion
PTA	Parent Teacher Association
SBM	School Business Manager
SEA	Strategic Executive Assistant
SEND	Special Education Needs and Disability
SENDCo	Special Education Needs and Disability Co-ordinator
SLT	Senior Leadership Team
TA	Teaching Assistant
VP	Vice Principal

Thanks from Jo Deane

Well - where to start! With Kimberley of course! I had never imagined that I would ever write a book (after all, who is really interested in what I have to say - right?) It took a little while for me to find my voice and Twitter (X) was an outlet that seemed to work for me. Once I had built up a small group of followers and a couple of individuals who would actively comment and re-tweet my stuff, a good balance of conversations and comments started to appear. I seemed to get a lot of activity from my posts and a few well respected people mentioned 'you should write a book'. It's one of those cliche phrases that a lot of the time, is just a throwaway comment - 'you should be on the TV!' But something just stuck in my head - maybe I really should have a go at writing a book! A book like this was never on my bucket-list or something I had a natural 'drawing' to but as time went on, I realised that if I had had a book like this when I started on my journey as a PA, it would have helped me enormously. It's been quite therapeutic to write and to be able to capture lessons and memories that would have eventually faded over time.

Kimberley and I were first introduced by Patrick Ottley-O'Connor (Coach and Leadership Consultant) on Twitter (X). From the first time Kimberley and I chatted, I knew we clicked. Once I got thinking, the writing seemed to flow. I knew that my work would be proofed – and I wasn't alone on this journey! Kimberley and I have spookily similar family and job histories. You could say the planets were aligned for us to collaborate on something together. Thank you Kimberley!

I had met Patrick lots of times virtually and in person, via Richard Uffendell. Patrick has a wealth of experience and always has good advice and is very well connected - thank you Patrick. Even when he is travelling the world with his wife Mel, he is unfailingly 'available' and has an unrivalled wisdom! Patrick emphasises that whatever is going on and however you are feeling at a given time, it's probably for a reason, and the journey you undertake will be worth the reward in the end. Most of all, Patrick is the living proof that your personal wellbeing is what matters above all else. 'Apply your own oxygen mask first, before helping others'.

I must thank the recruitment team who appointed me in my very first PA role in a school. Even though I feel like all my career had in some way been leading to this job, it was Ashton Park School who gave me an 'in'. They also sowed the seeds that allowed me to realise my worth, and my skill. Until then, I knew I was highly organised (and my family nick-named me Monica), but I didn't really give this a great deal of acknowledgement. Something that will always stick with me in the early days is when I received the feedback - 'I've never worked with anyone like you'. Thank you!

Headteacher Number 2 - Richard Uffendell. To say I have learned a lot (and continue to learn) from Richard is a pretty big understatement. Even during the Headteacher recruitment process, I was gaining experience that would normally never be afforded to an EA. Once appointed, Richard shared with me a new style of leadership, his unique style along with a vast breadth of knowledge, resources and connections. I felt as though I had been invited to the exclusive party! He brought (and continues to bring) a vision and humility to our school which is unparalleled in any school I have visited, and it is often commented on by external visitors, parents and even the students. He also saw my continued dedication and expertise in my role and instigated a further Job Evaluation which afforded me my current title of Strategic Executive Assistant. Richard introduced me to Stoicism too. A concept I knew little about, however once I had scratched beneath the surface slightly, I was hooked on the teachings of many great ancient Greek philosophers. On meeting Richard's family and him meeting mine, I could tell our collaborative work together would be a long and trusted relationship. Thank you Mr Uffendell.

My friends have always been important to me and I'm fortunate to have a bunch of Superhero friends who have been in my life for many years (some for over 40 years!) They've seen it all, the good, the bad and the ugly and still they come back for more. When I suggested to my mates that I was thinking of writing a book, without exception, they all said 'well of course you are - that's amazing'. They didn't appear to be surprised at all. This cemented to me that perhaps writing is something I could do. Their belief in me was more than my own self-belief - one of those times in life where I needed to listen intently and allow that belief to fill my soul. To Karen, Louise, Lynne, Nic, Sarah P, Sarah H - Thank you.

I must mention here a group of wonderful and inspirational people who are Bristol Fashion Chorus, who are part of the Ladies Association of British Barbershop Singers (LABBS). I joined the chorus in the Summer of 2023 and after a successful audition was welcomed into a very special and skilled group of singers under the direction and vision of Musical

Director Craig Kehoe. Never has a 'hobby' been so purposeful and rewarding for me, and at the time of writing (Autumn 2024), Craig has successfully led us to achieve our highest ranking to date of 4th in the LABBS Annual National Competition. A truly inspirational leader.

None of this would have been possible without the unfailing love and support of my Husband Gavin (of over 20 years), and our two children Zach and Alex. To them, I will be eternally grateful that I was given the time and energy to invest in myself these last few years, but also all the love and support we have given each other over our 30 year bond. The strength Gavin gives me (especially at times when I didn't/don't have any) is strong and unwavering. Thank you.

Thanks from Kimberley Evans

I don't remember particular conversations from my parents about self confidence or particular times when they encouraged me to find my path. I think in the 80s and 90s it was a lot more subtle than now (and my memory is really bad!), but whatever they did most definitely worked. For it's them that I have to thank for the attitude I have to life of 'give it a go!' and not letting a fear of failure stop me from living a full and adventurous life. They certainly taught me how to pack as much into a week as humanly possible, so Alistair and Sheila Oag - thank you for everything!

My passion for life is what drives me in life and although it is ridiculously busy, it is also ridiculously fun. I must thank my husband Gavin (a different one to Jo's I might add!) for putting up with my ideas and the rollercoaster they take us on. For supporting me to live my life in the way I want to and for loving me no matter what.

My love of writing was always simmering as I grew up, but it was my friend Kelly who made me a writer. As university students we became editors of our campus newspaper, The Bulletin, and as it was often hard to find contributors we ended up writing many, many articles ourselves. Looking back this was one of the early signs of what was to come - being heavily involved in community projects that fill my life with joy. 29 years later, I'm still best friends with Kelly and also Jenny from those amazing days at Bulmershe in Reading. Although they live far away, they still provide an amazing amount of support on my bad days and celebrate my good days with me. Our families have that special bond that when we are all together we laugh till we literally cry and don't even remember what was funny in the first place. The Llevans, my Inner Circle, you are my rock.

My daughters, Holly and Sophie, and their unique and special personalities, are what drives me. The reason I haven't got a 'proper' job is not only just because of them, but for them. To show them that there is more to the world than a traditional 9-5 job, that you don't have to stick to one career all your life and you can and should follow your dreams. Thank you girls for pushing me to be better, every single day.

I need to thank the universe for bringing Jo into my life, but this book happened because of the other things I have talked about above.

When Patrick Ottley-O'Connor linked the two of us up, that was the consequence of many, many events. Of me being on Twitter in the first place, because I was forging my own path in the world of business, because I am always up for trying new things and taking on new challenges. Being open to new opportunities and having the confidence to say yes to them. That's down to my parents, my friends and family all giving me the tools to do that.

I was well up for writing another book with Jo, but this has been so, so much more than that. I've gained an amazing friend who understands me on such a deep level it is like she has known me all my life.

Thank you Jo for putting your trust in me to write this with you, for understanding when I needed a break from it and allowing it to fit in around our lives and their dramas and hilarities. But also for pushing me when I needed it and being the energy when mine was down.

This may be the end of this project, but it's just the start of our adventures together.

Printed in Great Britain
by Amazon

50431038R00150